IT'S M

FOLLOW IN THE FOOTSTEPS OF
CHRISTIANS WHO IMPACTED THEIR WORLD

It's My Turn. Follow in the Footsteps of Christians Who Impacted Their World

Kingdom Building Ministries

ISBN No. 978-0-9819403-2-8

©2009 by Kingdom Building Ministries. All rights reserved.

Published by KBM Media, a division of Kingdom Building Ministries,

14485 E. Evans Ave., Aurora, Colorado 80014.

Scripture references from the Holy Bible, New International Version (NIV).

©1973, 1978, 1984, International Bible Society. Used by permission of Zondervan Bible Publishers.
Bold lettering indicates emphasis added by the authors.

Written, Researched and Complied by Amy Kannel
Edited by Mark Vermillion
Book/Cover design by Chris Turner.

Visit us online at www.kbm.org.

CONTENT

INTRODUCTION ›› WHY IS IT MY TURN NOW?   5

CHAPTER 1 ›› **KEITH GREEN**
IT'S MY TURN TO LOVE GOD INTIMATELY AND DEEPLY   9

CHAPTER 2 ›› **JOSIAH HENSON**
IT'S MY TURN TO SACRIFICE MYSELF FOR GOD AND OTHERS   13

CHAPTER 3 ›› **FLORENCE NIGHTINGALE**
IT'S MY TURN TO SERVE OTHERS WITH HUMILITY   19

CHAPTER 4 ›› **C.T. STUDD**
IT'S MY TURN TO OBEY GOD WITH RECKLESS ABANDON   23

CHAPTER 5 ›› **AMY CARMICHAEL**
IT'S MY TURN TO DIE TO MYSELF   27

CHAPTER 6 ›› **JOHN HYDE**
IT'S MY TURN TO INTERCEDE FOR THE LOST   31

CHAPTER 7 ›› **GEORGE MULLER**
IT'S MY TURN TO LIVE BY FAITH   35

CHAPTER 8 ›› **MARTIN LUTHER**
IT'S MY TURN TO STAND FOR TRUTH   41

CHAPTER 9 ›› **WATCHMAN NEE**
IT'S MY TURN TO SHARE IN CHRIST'S SUFFERING   45

CHAPTER 10 ›› **WILLIAM WILBERFORCE**
IT'S MY TURN TO RUN THE RACE OF FAITH AND PERSEVERANCE   51

CHAPTER 11 ›› **SUSANNA WESLEY**
IT'S MY TURN TO ADVANCE THE KINGDOM
IN THE ROLE UNIQUELY DESIGNED FOR ME   55

CHAPTER 12 ›› **ERIC LIDDELL**
IT'S MY TURN TO USE MY GOD-GIVEN GIFTS FOR HIS GLORY   61

CONTENT

CHAPTER 13 ›› DWIGHTY MOODY
IT'S MY TURN TO SHARE THE GOSPEL   67

CHAPTER 14 ›› WILLIAM CAREY
IT'S MY TURN TO BLESS THE NATIONS   71

CHAPTER 15 ›› DAWSON TROTMAN
IT'S MY TURN TO REPRODUCE OTHER LABORERS   75

THE LABORERS DECLARATION   80-81

CONCLUSION: A FINAL WORD OF CAUTION   83

APPENDIX ›› WHAT IS A LABORER?   87

BIBLIOGRAPHY   91

INTRODUCTION
FIRST THING'S FIRST

RELAY RACES ARE WON OR LOST at the handoff of the baton. In the same way, Christianity has survived nearly two thousand years because of millions of successful baton handoffs. Christ handed off His message of new life and servanthood to His disciples. They in turn handed it off to a few thousand believers. Those thousands went out and passed on the good news to the entire known world during the first century.

But the message would have been lost if it had not been continually passed on from generation to generation, century to century. Now, it's your turn. The baton is in your hands! Will you carry Christ's message into the next generation?

A BIBLICAL PERSPECTIVE
This book is about fifteen faithful "runners" who not only passed on their faith, but lived it out in a real, vibrant way. And as we observe the lives of these believers, they can serve as our mentors! In fact, mentoring is one of the most effective methods of passing on the baton. It's the way Christ and His disciples have shared their faith for centuries, and it simply involves living out your faith in front of those around you.

The Apostle Paul demonstrated this principle when he wrote to the believers in Corinth. "Therefore I urge you to imitate me," he said (1 Corinthians 4:16). Later in the same letter, Paul wrote, "Follow my example, as I follow the example of Christ" (1 Corinthians 11:1).

Most often, mentoring happens between two people who are both living, who can interact and talk together. But the writer of Hebrews recognized the power of historical mentoring—looking to role models or "heroes of the faith" as examples to follow. In Hebrews 11, we have one of the most amazing lists in the Bible. These men and women of faith, both named and unnamed, serve as ongoing illustrations of the benefits of selling out to God and living by faith. Hebrews 12 continues with an exhortation to persevere, reminding us of the "great cloud of witnesses" who have gone before us.

But the real power of historical mentoring is captured in the final chapter of the book of Hebrews: "Remember your leaders, who spoke the word of God to you. Consider the outcome of their way of life and imitate their faith" (Hebrews 13:7).

Wrapped up in this verse are three practical applications to the subject of heroes, role models, and historical mentors.

First we are told, "Remember your leaders." Too often we fail to see ourselves in connection with the rest of humanity throughout all of history. We view today as an isolated moment in time rather than a continuation of God's sovereign plan to reconcile the world to Himself. This isolation keeps us from relating meaningfully to the great heroes of faith who have gone before us. We have robbed ourselves of some of the most powerful role models and mentors we could ever hope to have.

Imagine it! With just a trip to the library or the bookstore, you can learn the secrets of doing great things for God from some of the greatest heroes of the Christian faith. During the prime of their lives, only a handful of people could get close to them. Most people have a fairly small inner network of confidants who spend time with them, share their heart, and participate in their struggles of faith. But today, we can enter into their lives. We can read entries from their journals, sit in their meetings, and observe them in their most vulnerable moments. To do so, we must first remember our leaders.

Second, we are challenged to "Consider the outcome of their way of life." Many of the sacrifices on the road to greatness in God's eyes are only brought into perspective when viewed from the end, looking back. You've heard the old saying, "Hindsight is 20/20." Often the choices we make in life can only be accurately evaluated when looking back on them. We can see both the consequences of mistakes and the benefits of positive decisions. When we're no longer in the moment, we can know results—it brings a proper sense of balance and perspective to the journey.

A classic illustration of this truth comes from the life of a man named C.T. Studd (his biography appears in chapter four). Born in the 1800s, C.T. grew up in a wealthy family in England and made a name for himself through his athletic ability playing cricket (a British version of baseball). He later shocked the world of cricket by answering the call of Hudson Taylor and sailing for China as a missionary.

While in China, this twenty-five-year-old missionary received final confirmation of the inheritance he knew would be coming from his father's fortune. By today's standards, he was independently wealthy—he would never need to work or raise support for his mission work again.

C.T. had prayed much about his inheritance and was convinced that God wanted him to seize the opportunity to do what the rich young ruler in Luke 18 had failed to do. On January 13, 1887, C.T. gave away his fortune. No one could have anticipated the results—in the eyes of the world, he was a fool. But now we can easily see the outcome of his way of life.

He gave 5,000 pounds to D.L. Moody (chapter twelve), an evangelist who had been instrumental in the conversion of C.T.'s father. Moody took that money and began a training center in Chicago, now known as Moody Bible Institute. C.T. sent another 5,000 pounds to George Müller (chapter six), who was doing extraordinary work among orphans in England. He sent 8,400 pounds to the Salvation Army, an organization working among the outcasts of London and beyond. And the list goes on! Countless people and ministries were blessed through C.T. Studd's sacrificial giving. We see that now as we consider the outcome.

Third, we are urged to "Imitate their faith." Notice that we are not exhorted to imitate their lives. We are told to imitate their faith. Often we are tempted to imitate the actions of our heroes. We think we have to become just like them. But God has a race marked out just for you. It is the faith of others, not necessarily their actions, that is worthy of our imitation.

The people featured in this book are not perfect. By offering them as historical mentors, we aren't suggesting that everything they did was right, or that their theology was flawless. They were human—they sometimes made mistakes and bad choices. But that's what makes them real—that's what proves that anyone can do what they did! Draw out the good lessons that you can learn from their lives, and leave the rest. Imitate their faith.

IT'S YOUR TURN!
Remember your leaders. Consider the outcome of their way of life. Imitate their faith. These are powerful admonitions. But the real power of these truths rests on the very next verse: "Jesus Christ is the same yesterday and today and forever" (Hebrews 13:8).

You have probably heard that verse quoted many times. But rarely is it ever placed in its original context. Verses seven and eight of Hebrews 13 make up one complete paragraph, connected by one common thought. The entire point of verse eight is to emphasize that what God has done in the lives of believers who have gone before us, He is still prepared to do today through people like you. The God we serve today is the same God they served fifty or a hundred or five hundred years ago!

It's important that as you seek to learn from those who have gone before, you keep your eyes fixed on Jesus, "the author and perfecter of our faith" (Hebrews 12:2). Don't get too discouraged by measuring your faith against others. Although their examples can be valuable, ultimately Jesus is the one you must imitate. He "authored" your faith, and He promises to "perfect" it. If you focus on Him, you, too, can do valuable things to advance God's Kingdom!

We are called to live lives of purity, obedience, sacrifice, and faith. But we are not alone. We are surrounded by a great cloud of witnesses who have modeled this life of faith for us. As you remember them, consider the outcome of their way of life, and imitate their faith, you can write new chapters for future generations who will follow in your footsteps. It's your turn!

In the following pages, you will read biographical sketches of laborers who have gone before us. We have not presented their entire life story, but rather, a few examples that illustrate one aspect of what it means to be a laborer for Christ. (See Appendix A, "What is a Laborer?") Some of these believers may spark within you a passion to learn more from the Kingdom exploits for which they are noted. We have included a bibliography at the end of the book for additional reading, so that you can dig deeper into the lives of these historical mentors by reading a full biography about them.

Take the time to interact with these laborers. Whether you're studying this book with a group or on your own, think through the application questions and write down your answers. And take the action steps! These interactive sections are designed to assist you in clarifying your next steps in obedience to God.

One of the best ways to fully grasp new truth is to teach it to someone else. You may consider using this book as a resource for small-group interaction. Or you may wish to share what you are learning with a contemporary mentor. Mentoring is a powerful relational stimulus for spiritual growth. As you walk through this material and grow in your faith, the encouragement, counsel, and accountability of a mentor will be invaluable.

Finally, make a commitment to be a laborer—a committed, active follower of Christ. This book is not just for historical information or entertainment—it will challenge you to make a decision. You'll have the opportunity to affirm your desire to become a laborer in God's harvest field by signing "The Laborer's Declaration." Think through this decision—it's not a vow to make halfheartedly. But we encourage you to demonstrate your willingness to love and serve God and others by signing the declaration and committing to become a laborer for the Kingdom.

IT'S YOUR TURN!

KEITH GREEN
1954-1982

DECLARATION 1
IT'S MY TURN TO LOVE GOD INTIMATELY AND DEEPLY

ALL HIS LIFE, Keith Green had dreamed of success as a singer and songwriter. But once he became a Christian, Keith's music wasn't just about fame or success—music became a way for him to connect with his Savior. More than anything, he longed for intimacy with Christ.

The music that Keith wrote out of his ever-deepening relationship with God has touched the hearts of countless people. One popular chorus, "O Lord, You're Beautiful," came out of one of his times with the Father. "The Lord brought me right into the throne room, and I sang to Him and just worshipped," Keith said about the song. That passion to know Christ is reflected in the lyrics:

> O Lord, You're beautiful. Your face is all I seek.
>
> For when Your eyes are on this child, Your grace abounds to me...

Nothing was dearer to Keith than knowing God personally. And to him, worship meant more than just singing a few songs and offering a prayer or two. "If you praise and worship Jesus with your mouth and your life does not praise and worship him, there's something wrong," he once said.

As Keith grew in his faith, he became consumed with a desire to see others truly worship God and develop the same intimacy with the Lord that he was experiencing. He saw that while many people went to church or to Christian concerts, very few of them truly seemed passionate about Christ. Keith was burdened by the idea of how that must grieve God, and he wanted to do something about it.

One year when he sang at "Jesus Northwest," a huge Christian music festival, he sensed that the whole event was nothing more than a party. The crowds were enjoying great music, but no one had really challenged them to draw near to God. When it was his turn to take the stage, Keith brought a tough message to the audience. He quoted a passage of Scripture from Amos and told them that God hated their festivals—what He really wanted was their hearts. Keith urged the people to fall in love with Jesus, and thousands got on their faces before the Lord.

In 1979, Keith experienced a personal revival, and his fervor swept through the group of people closest to him. He focused on the way that God grieves over "lukewarm" Christians, and he believed that God wanted to take the spirit of revival across the nation. The perfect place to start seemed to be in Tulsa, Oklahoma, where Keith's next concert was scheduled. He felt God's calling to present not just one concert, but a whole week of services on the campus of Oral Roberts University.

Once he received permission from the ORU administration to hold three evening programs, Keith began preparing for the work that he was sure God wanted to do. The first two evenings seemed successful, as many people responded to his messages. But he was not satisfied—he believed God was going to move powerfully in Tulsa and bring about a city-wide revival.

The third evening, ORU's Mabee Center was packed with nearly 4,500 people. Keith fasted and prayed all day, listening for the message God wanted him to present that night.

After opening with praise and worship and welcoming the presence of God, Keith brought before the crowd a list of sins God had told him were present on the campus. He challenged the audience members to confess their sins, reminding them of the pain they were causing Christ. A flood of individuals streamed forward to kneel or lie on their faces before God. As they came, Keith played the piano, not watching to see what was happening, but focusing on the Lord. He tearfully called for God to send His Spirit and break the hearts of everyone present.

Keith opened the microphone to anyone who had something they felt they needed to confess. Many made their way down the packed aisles to the front. Admissions of not supporting the ORU administration, false Christianity and breaking curfew led to emotional confessions of drug use and sexual immorality. With each confession came a deeper and more overwhelming sense of the nearness of the Spirit of God in the auditorium.

Meanwhile, Keith had crawled under the piano to get on his knees and worship God, praising Him for His presence. He didn't want to be in the spotlight or to interfere with the movement of the Spirit. In his times of worship and relationship with the Lord, he had aligned his heart with God's and had correctly heard the Holy Spirit. Revival came to ORU as a result of Keith's obedience and service born out of worship and intimacy with the Lord.

In addition to his music, Keith shared his passion with the body of Christ by speaking and writing through Last Days Ministries, the organization he founded with his wife, Melody. When he was only twenty-eight, he and two of his children were killed in a plane crash. At his memorial service, Melody said, "I know that Keith is where he wanted to be most. His heart was so with the Lord—he just had such a desire and burning to be close to Jesus. And he really didn't care about this life!"

> *"ONE THING I ASKED GOD FOR IN THAT PRAYER TIME WAS HIS HEART. THAT'S THE ONLY THING I NEEDED FROM HIM."*

SIGNIFICANT CONTRIBUTION

Keith Green's public ministry through writing, teaching, and music challenged the Church to go beyond spiritual apathy and embrace deep intimacy with God. He used his musical talents to inspire people to develop passionate faith, and he left a legacy of songs that speak of his love relationship with his Lord.

FOCUS SCRIPTURE

"Love the Lord your God with all your heart and with all your soul and with all your mind. This is the first and greatest commandment." (Matthew 22:37-38)

THINK ABOUT IT...

1. Read Matthew 22:34-40. Why do you think Jesus named this as the greatest commandment? How does a person's love for God affect other areas of his or her life?

2. How did Keith Green's intimate relationship with God strengthen his ministry at Jesus Northwest and at Oral Roberts University?

APPLY IT...

3. What does it mean to worship God? Search the Bible for Scriptures that can help you define the concept of worship.

4. Keith said, "If you praise and worship Jesus with your mouth and your life does not praise and worship him, there's something wrong." How can you praise and worship God with your life and not just your mouth?

5. Why is it so important to spend time cultivating your relationship with God? What are some practical ways you can do this?

TAKE ACTION!

Schedule an extended time alone with God—an hour, an afternoon, maybe even a whole day. You can spend the time praying, meditating on Scripture, journaling, listening to worship music, resting in God's presence—whatever helps you draw near to Him. Tell someone who can hold you accountable to following through with your plan.

JOSIAH HENSON
1789-1883

DECLARATION 2
IT'S MY TURN TO SACRIFICE MYSELF
FOR GOD AND OTHERS

JOSIAH HENSON DIDN'T SET OUT TO BE FAMOUS. In his early years, he was known only to his family and to his master. But after Harriet Beecher Stowe read his memoirs, he became the inspiration for the main character in her novel Uncle Tom's Cabin, which President Lincoln credited with starting the Civil War. Like the character in the book, Josiah longed to be free—and he risked his freedom to serve others.

Born into slavery in Maryland, Josiah found Christ through his mother, who often quoted Scriptures to him. She sent Josiah to a house meeting led by John McKenny, a nearby preacher. There, he heard a sermon on Hebrews 2:9—"That [Jesus] by the grace of God should taste death for every man" (KJV)—and he was elated to understand Christ's love and sacrifice for him.

Soon after, Josiah knew instinctively that God had him on a mission, and he determined to help whomever he could in life. He even sacrificed for those who kept him in slavery! Once when his master got into a drunken brawl, Josiah defended him and was repaid by having another white man break both his shoulder blades. He prayed for his masters, feeling sorry that they didn't know the love of Christ. And he refused to run away, believing it would be disloyal and would compromise his integrity.

Even though he hadn't been formally educated, Josiah also began to preach the Gospel, learning by listening to other great preachers. During a trip between his home in Maryland and his master's brother's plantation in Kentucky, he was ordained in the Methodist Episcopal Church and began preaching to raise funds and buy his freedom. But his master tricked him, and worse, he was soon taken to be sold in the Deep South.

Josiah's faith faltered. He felt that God had forsaken him, and during the trip down the river, he decided to kill his traveling companions and escape. But as he raised his ax to kill Amos Riley Jr., his master's nephew, he suddenly realized what he was about to do. "I shrunk back, laid down the axe, and thanked God, as I have done every day since, that I had not committed murder," he wrote in his memoirs. "[I then made] a solemn resolution to resign myself to the will of God, and take with thankfulness, if I could, but with submission, at all events, whatever he might decide should be my lot." And before Josiah could be sold, God intervened. Amos fell sick, and Josiah returned to Kentucky, nursing him back to health.

After that, Josiah decided to rescue himself and his family from slavery once and for all. They crossed the Ohio River, with Josiah carrying his two- and three-year-old sons over his shoulders in a homemade knapsack. This was incredibly painful, as his shoulders had never properly healed after being broken years before.

The Henson family nearly starved as they traveled across the Ohio wilderness on foot, and the skin on Josiah's back was completely worn after carrying his sons in a pouch for so long. When they finally arrived at Lake Erie, a ship captain agreed to take them to Buffalo, where they could cross to Canada and be free at last. Josiah was overcome with gratitude at the captain's generosity. When they arrived in Buffalo, he promised the captain, "I'll use my freedom well; I'll give my soul to God."

After forty-one years of slavery, Josiah was a free man—but his family had nothing. He found employment in Fort Erie, where he rented and cleaned out an old pigsty for the family to live in. He worked hard to gain his employer's respect, and he obtained livestock for his family. "I felt that my toils and sacrifices for freedom had not been in vain," he said. His labors to improve the lives of himself and others had not been wasted.

In Canada, however, he quickly saw that other former slaves were too easily satisfied—they had no understanding of what was within their grasp and had not improved their lives much. They didn't realize that they could become independent. But they looked to Josiah as a leader, and he began urging them to buy land of their own.

Soon Josiah helped build a permanent settlement and refuge for former slaves in the town of Dawn, Ontario. And he became a prominent speaker in the anti-slavery movement. His life story was published in 1849, and he traveled to Europe, where he met Queen Victoria and spoke ninety-nine times in England and Scotland.

But simply talking about abolition was not enough. "After I had tasted the blessings of freedom, my mind reverted to those whom I knew were groaning in captivity, and I at once proceeded to take measures to free as many as I could," he said. Though he faced enormous risk in returning to the United States to rescue others—if captured, he could be forced back into slavery—he longed to help others find the freedom he enjoyed. His first journey involved leaving his family and his safety and walking four hundred miles in order to lead a friend's family to freedom.

Eventually, Josiah helped free 118 slaves through the Underground Railroad. Knowing that he had played a vital part in delivering so many people from the cruel hand of slavery was "one of the greatest sources of my happiness," he said.

Josiah Henson traveled to preach the Gospel and speak out against slavery up to the very end of his life. He shared his hope in Christ with countless others, who found freedom from slavery and from sin because of his enormous sacrifices.

"IN THE COURSE OF MY PREACHING I TRIED TO IMPRESS UPON THEM THE IMPORTANCE OF THE OBLIGATIONS THEY WERE UNDER; FIRST, TO GOD, FOR THEIR DELIVERANCE; AND THEN, SECONDLY, TO THEIR FELLOW-MEN, TO DO ALL THAT WAS IN THEIR POWER TO BRING OTHERS OUT OF BONDAGE."

SIGNIFICANT CONTRIBUTION

After four decades as a slave, Josiah Henson became a well-known writer, preacher, abolitionist, and conductor in the Underground Railroad. He led his family to freedom, then went to great lengths to ensure the freedom and future happiness of more than one hundred other slaves. Josiah demonstrated selfless love for family, friends, and strangers by putting their freedom above his own comfort and safety.

FOCUS SCRIPTURE

"Greater love has no one than this, that he lay down his life for his friends." (John 15:13)

THINK ABOUT IT...

1. Read John 15:12-13. How does laying down your life for your friends demonstrate the greatest kind of love?

2. How do you think Josiah felt about leaving his family and risking his freedom in order to save others? What motivated him to make such a big sacrifice?

APPLY IT...

3. What does your willingness or unwillingness to lay down your life for someone else say about the depth of your love? How could laying down your life for someone affect your understanding and acceptance of the depth of Christ's love for you?

4. You may not be called to give up your physical life for others, but what are some ways you might figuratively "lay down your life" in sacrifice to show Christ's love to others?

5. On his trip down the river, Josiah felt that God had forsaken him. Have you ever felt that way? How can you fight this lie and be comforted by the truth that God will never leave you or forsake you?

6. Josiah recognized that all people are slaves to sin, so he helped people escape oppression from both the "sin of slavery and slavery of sin." How is sin a type of slavery? How can you find freedom from the slavery of sin, and how can you help others find that freedom?

TAKE ACTION!
According to 1 John 3:16-18, our love is proven to be real when it is displayed not just in words, but in actions. Think of one person you could lay your life down for this week, and show Christ's love to that person by sacrificing in some way to serve and help them.

IT'S MY TURN ›› FOLLOW IN THE FOOTSTEPS OF CHRISTIANS WHO IMPACTED THEIR WORLD

FLORENCE NIGHTINGALE

1820-1910

DECLARATION 3
IT'S MY TURN TO
ASSUME THE ROLE OF A SERVANT

IT WOULD HAVE BEEN EASY for an upper-class girl like Florence Nightingale—the attractive and popular daughter of a prominent English banker—to overlook the plight of the sick and the poor. Her sheltered life was filled with social events and mindless activities, and most of the wealthy people she associated with paid no attention to the suffering around them. But Florence couldn't ignore those less fortunate than she. She sensed God calling her to serve Him, though she didn't know how. And after sixteen long years, she was finally able to devote her life to God's work by entering the profession of nursing.

When Florence decided to become a nurse, it was far from a respectable move—in fact, her family was horrified and forbade her to pursue it. At that time, nurses were seen as careless and dirty, and they were infamous for immorality and drunkenness. And working conditions were terrible. The smell in most hospitals in the mid-1800s was unbearable from the dirt and the lack of hygiene; the nursing system was chaotic and largely ineffective.

Despite all these challenges, Florence believed that God had called her to be a nurse. She was so moved by the troubles of the sick and dying in England that she was determined to help them, no matter what the cost. She wanted to transform the profession—so she secretly studied any bit of information she could find about hospitals, eager to learn all she could about nursing and administration.

In 1853, Florence finally had the opportunity to fulfill her calling when she became Superintendent of London's Institution for the Care of Sick Gentlewomen in Distressed Circumstances. She made many changes to the hospital, and her loving service as a nurse earned her admiration from patients and the poor. Florence would often rub patients' feet if they were cold, or use her personal funds to send women to the seashore to recuperate.

Meanwhile, Britain was fighting the Crimean War in the Middle East, and an item in the London Times about the war caught Florence's attention. "...No sufficient preparations have been made for the proper care of the wounded," it said. "Not only are there no dressers and nurses...Men (are) kept in some cases for a week without the hand of a medical man..." The article ended with the challenge, "Are there no devoted women amongst us able...to go forth to minister to the sick and suffering soldiers? Are none...ready for such a work of mercy?" Florence's heart was stirred. Her longtime friend Sidney Herbert, the Secretary of War, asked her to pull together a group of nurses and go to the Crimea immediately.

She and almost forty other nurses responded to the call, and the conditions they found were horrible. A temporary hospital set up in a dirty, rundown barracks had no kitchen, no linen, no beds, no cups, no chairs, and no operating tables. The wounded stretched for four miles, with patients lying only a foot or two apart. Rats, maggots, and fleas were everywhere; the roof leaked; there were no lamps or candles or running water. Most soldiers who died didn't just die from their original wounds or diseases, but from the diseases they contracted in the dirty hospital. And the hospital was completely disorganized and inefficient— activities required too much paperwork, and Florence faced opposition from stubborn administrators who resented her expertise.

Immediately, she worked to develop a system for nursing the wounded while formulating plans to secure beds, bandages, cleaning supplies, clothing, eating utensils, and proper ventilation for the hospital. Often, she used her own money or solicited donations from friends in England to purchase needed supplies. Within weeks, amazing differences could be seen in the sanitary conditions of the hospital and the morale and health of the wounded.

In the midst of all the reform and administration, Florence's first commitment was still to the patients she served. "Christ is the author of our profession," she said, and she saw it as her duty to serve and care for the sick, giving them hope as He had done. Florence spent hours in the wards looking after patients. Often she could be found at the beds of the most severe cases, comforting and encouraging those deemed hopeless by the doctors, nursing them back to health, and saving limbs scheduled for amputation.

The men saw her as an angel. The London Times reported, "When all the medical officers have retired for the night and silence and darkness have settled down upon those miles of prostrate sick, she may be observed alone, with a little lamp in her hand, making her solitary rounds."

Florence Nightingale rose to a position of respect and authority because of her resources, her calm, caring spirit, and her ability to make significant changes in the nursing system. But she resisted all the accolades and recognition that came her way. At the end of the war, she stayed at the hospital for a few months to nurse the remaining soldiers until they, too, could return home. A British war ship was provided for her return, and England prepared for her arrival with brass bands and ceremonies. Florence had other plans. Using an assumed name, she booked passage on a small steamer for the trip to England. She traveled by train as an unknown passenger, walked home from the train station, and entered her home unannounced, through the back door.

> *"OH, LORD, THOU PUTTEST INTO MY HEART THIS GREAT DESIRE TO DEVOTE MYSELF TO THE SICK AND SORROWFUL. I OFFER IT TO THEE."*

SIGNIFICANT CONTRIBUTION

Florence Nightingale used a vision for Christian service to transform the nursing profession into a respectable field that provided invaluable care for the sick and wounded. In addition to her humble and devoted work with patients, she wrote a monumental book called Notes on Nursing, considered a valuable guide to the profession. Because of her caring service to the sick and poor, her innovative reform of the nursing system, and her book, she has been called "the mother of modern nursing."

FOCUS SCRIPTURE

"Your attitude should be the same as that of Christ Jesus: Who, being in very nature God, did not consider equality with God something to be grasped, but made himself nothing, taking the very nature of a servant, being made in human likeness." (Philippians 2:5-7)

THINK ABOUT IT...

1. Read Philippians 2:1-11. Identify the characteristics that Paul mentions in this passage to describe a humble servant.

2. What specific attitudes or actions do you think of when you imagine a person who humbly looks out for the interests of others?

APPLY IT...

3. Would those around you characterize you as a person who looks out for the interests of others? Why or why not?

4. Think of someone you know personally who exemplifies the servant-attitude that Florence Nightingale possessed. What do you admire about that person? How can you imitate his or her humility?

5. Florence believed that God had placed in her heart a desire to devote her life to the care of the sick. What desires has God placed in your heart? What small steps can you take today toward fulfilling those dreams or callings?

TAKE ACTION!

Think of a menial task you can do this week that will serve and bless someone. Do the task anonymously, and seek to cultivate a humble servant's heart by working cheerfully and giving up thoughts of praise and recognition.

C.T. STUDD

1862-1931

DECLARATION 4
IT'S MY TURN TO OBEY GOD WITH RECKLESS ABANDON

AT FIFTY YEARS OF AGE, C.T. Studd was not the prime candidate for a frontier missions thrust to the heart of unevangelized Africa. At least not from a human point of view. He had already served in China and India, helping lead the Cambridge Seven (a group of English university students who committed to go to China after hearing D.L. Moody preach) overseas in 1885 with China Inland Mission. He also toured American universities in the early stages of the Student Volunteer Movement, which mobilized more than twenty thousand college students as career missionaries! And C.T.'s health had been failing for fifteen years—his severe asthma alone was reason enough to keep him out of tropical Africa.

But in Liverpool, England, in 1908, C.T. noticed a sign that appealed to his curiosity and sense of humor. "Cannibals want missionaries," the sign proclaimed. Why, sure they do, for more reasons than one, C.T. thought. He was hooked—he had to go in and hear more.

Inside, Dr. Karl Krumm was telling of his experiences walking across Africa. Dr. Krumm explained that in the middle of the continent lived countless tribes who had never heard the story of Jesus Christ. Explorers, big-game hunters, traders, European officials, and scientists had all been to those regions—but no Christian had ever gone to tell of Jesus.

"The shame sank deep into one's soul," C.T. said. "Why have no Christians gone?" he wondered. God replied, "Why don't you go?" "The doctors won't permit it," C.T. said. God's answer came, "Am I not the Good Physician? Can I not take you through? Can I not keep you there?" C.T. had no excuses—he had been called to Africa.

He was in ill health and already beyond the prime of his life. But that would not deter him. He discussed a strategy with Dr. Krumm, and the two of them planned an exploratory journey to southern Sudan, a thousand miles south of Khartoum. The rapid spread of Islam in that area gave them both a sense of urgency to plant a chain of mission stations to stem the tide and instead share the gospel of Jesus Christ with the people.

C.T.'s next major need was for funding. He had long since given away any wealth he possessed, and he had no money left to go to Africa. He outlined the challenge to a group of businessmen, whom God rallied to back the project. But they presented one important qualifier: C.T. must see a doctor and be given medical clearance.

After examining him, the doctor told the businessmen that C.T. would die if he ventured south of Khartoum. He must agree to this restriction or no funds would be given. But he could never comply with such a limitation; it would undermine the entire project. He responded to the group of businessmen with these words: "Gentlemen, God has called me to go, and I will go. I will blaze the trail, though my grave may only become a stepping stone that younger men may follow."

It seemed crazy—a penniless, fifty-year-old man with asthma and malaria, bent on going to the heart of Africa. But C.T. had learned that God laughs at impossibilities. His years of service under the leadership of Hudson Taylor and the China Inland Mission had taught him that in the crucible of life, God could be trusted. He would proceed by faith.

Sure enough, God provided the supplies, and C.T. went on the exploratory mission. While in Sudan, he heard about masses of people in the Belgian Congo who had never heard of Christ. That settled it—C.T. could never spend the remainder of his years in England, when Africans had such a desperate need for the Gospel.

The exploratory mission came to a close, and C.T. returned to England aflame with a vision for this New Crusade. He traveled to Cambridge and gave a passionate plea on behalf of the unreached peoples in the heart of Africa. He also wrote powerful booklets that fueled the fires of his cause.

Before long, C.T. returned to Africa. The night before he left, he spoke with a young man who questioned his plans. "Is it a fact that at fifty-two, you mean to leave your country, your home, your wife, and your children? C.T. responded, "If Jesus Christ be God and died for me, then no sacrifice can be too great for me to make for Him." His words became the motto of the crusade.

C.T. Studd did die in Africa as the doctor predicted—only it was twenty years later! Through his faith and obedience in the face of great sacrifice, many thousands were brought into the Kingdom, and a new mission agency, Worldwide Evangelization Crusade International, was born. His last written words were, "Let God be magnified! Hallelujah!"

> *"SOME WISH TO LIVE WITHIN THE SOUND OF CHURCH OR CHAPEL BELL. I WANT TO RUN A RESCUE SHOP WITHIN A YARD OF HELL."*

SIGNIFICANT CONTRIBUTION

One of the fruits of C.T. Studd's radical obedience was the formation of the Heart of Africa Mission. Later known as WEC International, the Heart of Africa Mission was a new agency birthed out of his pioneer ministry among the unreached peoples of central Africa. Not only did C.T. answer God's call, he also mobilized others to radically obey God, challenging thousands to join him on the front lines of the battle for the spread of the gospel.

FOCUS SCRIPTURE

"This is love for God: to obey his commands. And his commands are not burdensome..." (1 John 5:3)

THINK ABOUT IT...

1. Read 1 John 5:2-4. How are obedience and love connected? Why do you think God places such a high value on obedience?

2. Do you think C.T. Studd felt that God's call to go to Africa was burdensome? Why or why not?

APPLY IT...

3. Do God's commands ever seem burdensome to you? Why or why not?

4. In what ways have you seen God "laugh at impossibilities," either in your own life or in the lives of others? Why do you think God likes to use unlikely people to accomplish His purposes?

TAKE ACTION!

Find an "unlikely laborer" in your church or school—someone whom the world might overlook, but who could influence their world for Christ. What one thing can you do to invest in them or call out their potential to have a powerful Kingdom impact? (Some examples: invite them to do ministry alongside you, take them out for lunch or coffee to encourage them, help them pull together the money to go to a camp or a retreat.)

AMY CARMICHAEL

1867-1951

DECLARATION 5
IT'S MY TURN TO DIE TO SELF

AMY CARMICHAEL WAS A FUN-LOVING YOUNG GIRL with an eye for beauty. But as she matured and grew in her faith, she began to realize that following Christ meant dying to self and to the things of this world. Her love for the Lord led her to India, where she served as mother and mentor to countless children and fellow workers. Time and again she put her own desires aside, crucifying her earthly nature so that she could live wholly for God.

Amy first learned about death to self at age seventeen, as she and her brothers were on their way home from church in Belfast, Ireland. They came across a poor old woman carrying a heavy bundle, and it seemed only right for them to take the bundle and help the woman. But they soon noticed that the "respectable people" of the community were staring at them. Amy felt ashamed to be publicly associated with such a woman, and she later wrote about how much she and her brothers hated the experience.

As they trudged on, though, a passage of Scripture from 1 Corinthians 3:12-14 suddenly came into Amy's mind: "[Now if any man build upon this foundation] gold, silver, precious stones, wood, hay, stubble; every man's work will be made manifest: for the day shall declare it, because it shall be declared by fire; and the fire shall try every man's work of what sort it is. If any man's work abide...[he shall receive a reward]" (KJV). The words were so real that Amy turned to see who had spoken them. She saw nothing, but she knew it had been the voice of God.

That afternoon, Amy did some serious soul-searching. She determined in her heart to follow Christ, even if it meant forsaking the luxury and beauty she enjoyed. From then on, she would be "dead to the world and its applause, to all its customs, fashions, laws."

As a teenager, Amy began to reach out to the "shawlies," girls who worked in the mills and were too poor to buy hats. They used their shawls to cover their heads, which was offensive to the proper church members. The church members were appalled that Amy would bring such "common" girls into the church, but Amy didn't care about her reputation. Christ was at work loving the shawlies through her.

To the relief of the church folk, the shawlies soon began coming in such large numbers that Amy needed a separate building for them. She trusted God to provide land and a building, and "The Mill and Factory Girls' Branch of the YWCA" was opened in 1889. A banner at the grand opening proclaimed, "That in all things He might have the preeminence." Others led the service that night; Amy wasn't even on the platform. Though it was her vision that initiated the ministry and her dream that made the building possible, she sat inconspicuously in the middle of the audience, seeking no recognition.

After much fruitful ministry at home, Amy decided to go overseas—but many people discouraged or mocked her. She understood more of what it might mean to die to self and be shamed for Christ's sake, and she found new meaning in the

Scriptures that talk about death to self and life in Christ. She wrote about being "dead to all one's natural earthly plans and hopes, dead to all voices, however dear, which would deafen our ear to His."

She persevered in her calling, and following a brief service in China, Amy settled in India, where she shared the Gospel and rescued children from prostitution in Hindu temples. Over the course of her ministry there, caring for children began to take up more and more of her time. It seemed less important or profitable than other work she might have done—but she gradually saw the value in offering herself to God for whatever He would have her do, even to serve as mother to His children. It wasn't her place to decide what work was more important—she was to be obedient to the Lord. She wrote, "If by doing some work which the undiscerning consider 'not spiritual work' I can best help others, and I inwardly rebel, thinking it is the spiritual for which I crave, when in truth it is the interesting and exciting, then I know nothing of Calvary love."

Over and over, she refused to question God. Each question was a chance to die, to be reminded of Christ's Lordship in her life. "He held all the rights. She had turned them over long ago to Him when she resolved to follow Him to the uttermost," said Elisabeth Elliot in her biography of Amy. "It was one more way of saying no to herself and yes to God."

Amy spent the rest of her life—more than fifty-three years—in India without a single furlough, setting up orphanages and ministering to the people she met. She also founded the Dohnavur Fellowship, a place of refuge for children. When it came to Christian service, the standards she set for herself and others were high—she didn't want any fellow workers who were not also prepared to die to self for the sake of the Gospel.

"O to be delivered from half-hearted missionaries!" she said. "Don't come if you mean to turn aside for anything—for the 'claims of society' in the treaty ports and stations. Don't come if you haven't made up your mind to live for one thing the winning of souls."

While serving in India, she received a letter from a young lady back home who was considering overseas missions. The girl asked, "What is missionary life like?" Amy Carmichael wrote back simply, "Missionary life is a chance to die."

> *"A CRUCIFIED LIFE CANNOT BE SELF-ASSERTIVE. THE CUP THAT IS FULL OF SWEET WATER CANNOT SPILL BITTER-TASTING DROPS, HOWEVER SHARPLY IT IS KNOCKED."*

SIGNIFICANT CONTRIBUTION

Amy Carmichael's life and ministry exemplified the heart of the Father who embraces the orphans, widows, and outcasts of society. She personified selflessness and humility and gave up everything for the sake of following Christ, rejecting the luxuries and comforts of her life in Ireland to be "mother" to children in India who desperately needed her. The Dohnavur Fellowship, which she founded, is still in operation today, and God used her to rescue thousands and give them hope in Christ.

FOCUS SCRIPTURE

"Then he said to them all: 'If anyone would come after me, he must deny himself and take up his cross daily and follow me. For whoever wants to save his life will lose it, but whoever loses his life for me will save it.'" (Luke 9:23-24)

THINK ABOUT IT...

1. Read Luke 9:23-25. What does it mean to lose your life for Christ?

2. When "The Mill and Factory Girls' Branch of the YWCA" was opened as a result of Amy's work, she was not in the spotlight—she didn't receive recognition or attention. How do you think she might have felt about this? What might have enabled her not to care about getting credit?

APPLY IT...

3. When Amy spent her time in India caring for children, she said, "If by doing some work which the undiscerning consider 'not spiritual work' I can best help others, and I inwardly rebel, thinking it is the spiritual for which I crave, when in truth it is the interesting and exciting, then I know nothing of Calvary love." Put her statement in your own words. What is some "unspiritual work" you could do that would help others and show Calvary love?

4. A turning point in Amy's life came when she was reminded of the words of 1 Corinthians 3:12-14. Think about the implications of this Scripture: Which materials will withstand fire? What are you building with? How can you build with the right materials?

5. Though we know that we should not care about our reputations, sometimes it's hard to ignore what other people think of us. How can you, like Amy, seek to live for Christ's approval and not for the applause and approval of the world?

TAKE ACTION!

For one week (or perhaps even one month), choose to sacrifice something of your own desires and replace that with an element of service or devotion to God. (Examples: turn off the television and use your TV-watching hours to spend time with God or serving others; give up junk food and give the money you spend on it to someone in need.) How can you, in the spirit of Amy Carmichael, develop a lifestyle pattern of giving up your earthly desires for the greater goal of dying to self and glorifying God?

JOHN HYDE

1865-1912

DECLARATION 6
IT'S MY TURN TO
INTERCEDE FOR THE LOST

THE PEOPLE OF INDIA called John Hyde "the man who never sleeps" because of his perseverance in prayer. He was slow of speech, slightly hearing impaired, meek, and mild-mannered. But his steadfast commitment to the power of prayer taught the missionaries and the people of India that prayer is the driving force behind God's work.

Just before the turn of the twentieth century, John sensed a call to minister to an unreached people group in the nation of India. He was one of only five missionaries to serve in the Punjab region, and they were persecuted by the natives, winning few converts early on. John realized that he would have to rely on the power of prayer, so he began to lead his fellow missionaries in intercession for the people of India.

In 1899, he began spending entire nights in prayer—after working all day, he would labor in prayer all night! Prayer for the lost became his passion, his primary focus in ministry. He understood the importance of intercession in aligning his heart with the sovereign God who would accomplish the work through him.

In 1904, John attended the first of what would become an annual convention for Indian Christians and Western missionaries. He helped form the Punjab Prayer Union to support the convention, convincing his fellow workers that nothing could happen for the Kingdom of God apart from intercessory prayer. The workers had seen so little fruit that they were easily convinced of this truth.

By the second year of the convention, John had gained a reputation as a man of prayer. He spent many days and nights in the prayer room, strengthened and sustained by God. As he prayed, he often became so heavy-hearted for the sins of the world and of the church that he would burst into tears. A friend of his wrote, "He missed many meals, and when I went to his room I would find him lying as in great agony, or walking up and down as if an inward fire were burning in his bones." Yet although he often went without sleep and food, John was joyful and energetic. "One thought was constantly uppermost in his mind," his friend wrote—"that our Lord still agonizes for souls."

John had a burden for souls, and at the 1908 convention, he dared to pray for what seemed like an impossible request: He asked God for one soul per day to be won to Christ. Though most of the other workers could not fathom such results, he went ahead with his bold request—and by the next year, over four hundred people had been won to Christ!

During the 1909 convention, John made a new prayer goal: He wanted to double the number of souls won. It seemed impossible again, but this time, his fellow Christians joined him in prayer. And sure enough, by the next convention, over eight hundred souls had been won! In that convention, he determined to double the goal again. He prayed with unquenchable passion: "O, God, give me souls or I die!"

It was then that John was nicknamed "Praying Hyde." Four souls a day was his new goal, and it was reached. Then he began to travel around India, convincing other workers and nationals to pray for the lost.

While John was in Calcutta, his health began to fail. Some of his friends talked him into seeing a doctor, and the doctor made a strange discovery. John's heart had shifted positions inside his body—it was now on the right side of his chest! Years of passionate labor in both prayer and calling others to pray had affected his frail body.

The doctor gave him strict instructions to get complete rest for several months or he would die. But "Praying Hyde" could not give up. He lived for two more years, continuing his passionate ministry of intercession, and he saw a wave of conversions that was unprecedented in that part of the world.

When John finally left India in 1911, he attended an evangelistic meeting in England, and he felt burdened to pray for the meeting. Dr. J. Wilbur Chapman, who was one of the speakers, wrote:

"The audience was extremely small, results seemed impossible but I received a note saying that an American missionary was coming to the town and was going to pray God's blessing upon our work. He was known as 'Praying Hyde.'

"Almost instantly the tide turned. The hall was packed, and my first invitation meant fifty men for Jesus Christ. As we were leaving I said, 'Mr. Hyde, I want you to pray for me.' He came to my room…dropped on his knees, waited five minutes without a single syllable coming from his lips. …Then with upturned face, down which the tears were streaming, he said: 'Oh, God!' Then for five minutes at least, he was still again, and then when he knew he was talking with God his arm went around my shoulder and there came up from the depth of his heart such petitions for men as I had never heard before. I rose from my knees to know what real prayer was."

Many were saved at those meetings. Afterwards, although John was very sick and his body was frail, he said, "The burden of Shrewsbury was very heavy, but my Saviour's burden took Him down to the grave."

He continued his ministry of intercession up to the time of his death, praying from his bed or wheelchair. And today, John Hyde stands as a testimony not to the power of gifts and intellect, but to the power of the Holy Spirit that comes when we intercede in prayer for the lost.

"O, GOD, GIVE ME SOULS OR I DIE!"

SIGNIFICANT CONTRIBUTION

John Hyde's missionary methods underscore the truth that prayer is the driving force behind world evangelization. Like the early apostles, John recognized that time in prayer and study of the Scriptures could not be compromised by other seemingly worthwhile activities. He pursued God's heart for the lost and interceded for thousands to enter the Kingdom of heaven.

FOCUS SCRIPTURE

"Devote yourselves to prayer, being watchful and thankful." (Colossians 4:2)

THINK ABOUT IT...

1. Read Colossians 4:2-4. What does it mean to be "watchful and thankful" in prayer?

2. John's prayer for one soul a day seemed impossible—
   but God went beyond that request for 365 souls and brought over 400! Read Ephesians 3:20. Why might it be valuable to pray for things that seem out of reach or farfetched?

APPLY IT...

3. It was John Hyde's initial "failure" (lack of conversions) that led to his fervent prayers. How have you seen failure inspire prayer? In what ways might God use failure to help you grow?

4. Have you ever felt a burden to pray for someone or something? What do you think might prompt God to lay such burdens on specific people?

TAKE ACTION!

John Hyde often missed meals in order to spend more time praying. Make a commitment to fast—perhaps just one meal, if it's your first time—and spend the extra time in prayer. You might also begin keeping a prayer journal to help you become more aware of God's answers to your prayers. Use the journal to record what you pray for and when and how God answers.

GEORGE MÜLLER

1805-1898

DECLARATION 7
IT'S MY TURN TO LIVE BY FAITH

THROUGHOUT HIS EARLY YEARS, George Müller denied the reality of God and lived in sin, simply going through the motions of religion. But his life turned around when a friend invited him to a college Bible meeting where the prayers were sincere and the sermon came alive. George asked God to make him a true Christian, and his bold faith in God soon became an example for many to follow.

He decided that he wanted to be a missionary, but his father opposed the idea, so George decided not to accept any more money from him, instead trusting God to provide for his needs. When he first needed money to live on, he asked God—and one hour later, a professor offered him a tutoring job that would pay four times the normal rate! When he couldn't afford his rent, he was soon offered a free room at a nearby orphanage. Those experiences taught him that God could be trusted.

George became a pastor in London, and before long, he gave up the income he received because it came from renting pews in the church, which he thought was wrong. He decided not to ask anyone for money, but instead, to trust God to supply his needs. And God always provided. George and his family gave away any extra money they had, never keeping what they didn't absolutely need and never borrowing.

In 1832, George moved to Bristol and began a Breakfast Club for needy children, inviting them to his house to share Scripture with them and trusting God to provide food. Soon forty children attended every morning. But George still felt he needed to do more to help children, and the opportunity came when God called him to start an orphanage.

Though many people discouraged the idea, saying it wouldn't work, he found a house to rent and scheduled the opening of his first orphanage in 1836. Soon it was home to twenty-six girls, with forty-two more on a waiting list. He hated turning children away, so he rented two more houses down the street. He and his staff were caring for eighty-one children, with enough on waiting lists to fill three more homes. And he also started the Scriptural Knowledge Institution for Home and Abroad, which established schools for the poor, purchased Bibles for the needy, and supported foreign missionaries.

George then decided to build one big orphanage in the country, believing that it would teach other Christians faith and show them how God answers prayer. The endeavor would require thirty-five thousand pounds—but he wrote, "The greatness of the sum required affords me a kind of secret joy; for the greater the difficulty to be overcome, the more will it be seen to the glory of God how much can be done by prayer and faith."

George's faith was vital in his ministry to the orphans, as he trusted God to meet the children's daily needs. One morning, over three hundred kids came to breakfast. The table was set, but there was no food. Nevertheless, George gave thanks for what God was going to give them to eat and told the children to sit down. He didn't know where their food would come from, but he knew that somehow, God would provide. Just then, a baker knocked at the door. He explained that the night before, he hadn't been able to sleep—so at two o'clock in the morning, he got up and made three batches of bread for the orphanage. A few moments later, a milkman knocked at the door. He had broken a wheel on his cart, and he needed to lighten his load—so he offered the orphanage ten full cans of free milk! George wrote in his journal, "The Lord not only gives as much as is absolutely necessary for His work, but He gives abundantly."

In his later years, George began preaching around the world. On one trip, the ship ran into thick fog just off the coast of Newfoundland. George needed to be in Quebec by Saturday afternoon to make his first speaking engagement—but the captain said it was impossible.

"If you cannot find a way to get me there on time, I'll have to ask God to do it," George responded. "I have not missed a single engagement in fifty-two years, and I don't intend to start now. Come down to my cabin with me, and we will pray together." The captain said, "What's the point of praying? The fog is so thick I cannot see to the stern. Take a look for yourself, Mr. Müller." But George simply said, "I don't need to look. My eye is not on the weather, but on the One who controls the weather!"

George began to pray: "Dear God, I come to You now to ask You to do the impossible. You know that I need to be in Quebec by Saturday and that the fog has hemmed us in. Please lift the fog so that the ship can go forward and I will be on time. Amen." Then he turned to the captain. "I have known my Lord for fifty-two years, and in all that time I cannot recall a single instance where he has not answered my prayers. I can assure you, the fog has lifted." Sure enough, the fog was completely gone! And by the time the ship docked, the captain had placed his faith in the God whom George trusted so completely.

By 1870, George Müller was operating five orphanages—caring for more than two thousand children! Yet he knew that the ministry did not rest on him. "When it is the Lord's pleasure to remove this servant from my post, people will see that it is I who was dependent on Him and not He who was dependent on me," George said. "He can and will easily raise up another servant, and...the orphan houses will continue to flourish."

> *"THE GREATER THE DIFFICULTY TO BE OVERCOME, THE MORE WILL IT BE SEEN TO THE GLORY OF GOD HOW MUCH CAN BE DONE BY PRAYER AND FAITH."*

SIGNIFICANT CONTRIBUTION

Because of his work in caring for ten thousand orphans, George Müller has been called "The Father of Homeless Waifs." He lived out his belief that "with God, no emergency is unseen and no want is unprovided for"—and as a result, his faith is a model for Christians to follow. His work continues today through the Müller Foundation, which cares for orphans, provides for the elderly, and contributes to the work of missionaries worldwide.

FOCUS SCRIPTURE

"And without faith it is impossible to please God, because anyone who comes to him must believe that he exists and that he rewards those who earnestly seek him." (Hebrews 11:6)

THINK ABOUT IT...

1. Read Hebrews 11. Why is it impossible to please God without faith? What stands out to you about the faith of the famous Bible characters listed in this chapter?

2. What are some obstacles to faith? How do you think George Müller might have overcome such obstacles?

APPLY IT...

3. George struggled to trust God for the provisions necessary to open an orphanage until he meditated upon Psalm 81:10: "I am the LORD your God, who brought you up out of Egypt. Open wide your mouth and I will fill it." How have you seen God provide for your needs in the past? How does remembering that change your perspective on the future?

4. What are some advantages and disadvantages of raising support, as many ministry organizations today do, versus asking no one for money and just praying that God will provide, as George Müller did?

5. After he began his work in Bristol, George had the opportunity to go to Baghdad as a missionary. But he realized that there were plenty of needy people in Bristol. "God has given me a mission field right here, and I will live and die in it," he said. What constitutes a mission field? What unconventional "mission fields" might be just around the corner from you?

TAKE ACTION!

George's work in serving and caring for orphans illustrates part of James 1:27 — "Religion that God our Father accepts as pure and faultless is this: to look after orphans and widows in their distress..." You may not be called to open an orphanage, but you can help provide for needy children is through organizations like Compassion International. Consider sponsoring a child in another country through Compassion. (If you don't have a lot of money, you could join with a group of friends to co-sponsor a child.) For more information, check out Compassion International's website at www.compassion.org.

MARTIN LUTHER

1483-1546

DECLARATION 8
IT'S MY TURN TO STAND FOR TRUTH

MARTIN LUTHER WAS A HUMBLE MONK who had no intentions of inciting a revolutionary movement within the church. But as he grew in his faith and understanding of God's Word, he began to see how society had strayed from the truth of Scripture. No matter what others said or did, he wanted to base his life and faith on God's unchanging Word—and he wanted those around him to do the same.

During his early years in the Roman Catholic Church, Martin anxiously confessed his sins before a priest for as long as six hours at a time. The Church taught that sins were forgiven only after confession, and Martin was desperate to receive God's mercy. But the more he confessed, the more he realized that he could never remember and confess every single sin, and he began to panic. It wasn't until 1518, when he had been a monk for ten years, that Martin finally understood the concept of salvation by faith, through God's grace.

As he meditated on Christ's sacrifice on the cross and read Scripture, he began to see the love of God. And as he studied the book of Romans, he began to grasp the idea of justification by faith. Romans 1:17 suddenly became clear: the righteousness that God demands through the law is provided through faith in Jesus Christ alone! The only requirement was faith to receive the perfect righteousness of Christ as payment for sin.

As Martin examined Church practices, he saw a lot of corruption. God's Word was not accessible to the common people, and many traditions were not founded on truth. As his understanding of theology grew, Martin became concerned about the legalism and materialism he saw. He wrote a list of "Ninety-Five Theses" about the problems and tacked it to the door of the Wittenburg Chapel in Germany. This was not a rebellious or radical act—in his day, it was the traditional method of inviting debate and discussion. But this list, along with some of Martin's other writings, led to the birth of the Reformation movement in Europe.

Martin continued to write several treatises calling for reforms within the Church, even though doing so brought increased pressure from Pope Leo X to recant or be excommunicated. One such treatise suggested restraints on the Pope's role and questioned the sale of indulgences. (Indulgences are a means of relieving the punishment or penalty for sin and lessening time spent in purgatory. At that time, the Pope was soliciting money that would be used to build a large cathedral in Rome. Christians who paid money to the Church would receive indulgences.)

Another treatise, "On the Freedom of the Christian," held that justification and the forgiveness of sins came through faith alone. The Church had associated forgiveness with laws, rules, politics, and indulgences. Eventually, Martin was excommunicated from the Church, and the archbishop ordered that his writings were to be burned.

In 1521, the emperor called for an imperial diet (trial) to meet in Worms, Germany, and determine Martin's fate. Many saw him as an outlaw because of his controversial writings and his boldness in challenging accepted Church practices.

As the diet began, Church officials showed Martin a large pile of books and asked him, "Did you write these books?" If he had been willing to claim ownership of only some of the books, focusing on indulgences and forgetting his protest against the seven sacraments, he might have led a movement uniting all of Germany against extortion and abuse of authority by the Pope. But he would not compromise. He said that he had written all of them, and the officials then asked, "Will you now take back all the things you said in these books?" Martin asked for time to consider the question, and the emperor allowed him one day to respond.

The next day, the trial drew large crowds, and Martin was asked the question again. He answered, "Unless I am convicted by Scripture and plain reason…my conscience is captive to the Word of God. I cannot and I will not recant anything, for to go against conscience is neither right nor safe. God help me. Amen." His statement sent shockwaves through the audience, and the fear of revolt by the people of Germany led Martin's strongest opponents to appeal to the emperor for a continued private hearing by a committee. But three days of questioning and appeals for him to change his stand were unsuccessful. He would not be moved.

After Martin's trial, the Edict of Worms proclaimed him a heretic and declared that he could be killed without penalty. Yet even then, he did not let danger deter him from working to make God's Word the foundation of truth for all people. In 1522, he translated the New Testament into German at a time when only scholars who knew Latin and Greek could read the Bible. And in 1534, he published a complete German Bible.

Years later, Martin wrote that the thought which consumed him during his trial was not that he was before an emperor, but that both he and the emperor would have to answer to God. The desire to stand unashamed before his heavenly Father gave him strength to stand unwavering before the earthly emperor. God's word was Martin Luther's final authority.

"I OWN BUT ONE THING, MY OWN UNWORTHY BODY…IF THEY CHOOSE TO TAKE IT…THEY WILL BUT MAKE ME POORER BY ONE OR TWO HOURS OF LIFE. THE SWEET REDEEMER, MY LORD JESUS CHRIST, IS ENOUGH FOR ME, TO WHOM I SHALL SING AS LONG AS I LIVE. AND IF ANYONE IS UNWILLING TO SING WITH ME, THEN WHAT IS THAT TO ME?"

SIGNIFICANT CONTRIBUTION

Martin Luther's "Ninety-Five Theses," tacked to the Wittenburg Chapel door, summarized his protest against the corruption in the Church and ushered in the Protestant Reformation of the early sixteenth century. His dedication to making God's truth accessible to all people led to his translation of the Bible into the German vernacular—the first German Bible translated directly from the original languages and containing common German vocabulary.

FOCUS SCRIPTURE

"To the Jews who had believed him, Jesus said, 'If you hold to my teaching, you are really my disciples. Then you will know the truth, and the truth will set you free.'"(John 8:31-32)

THINK ABOUT IT...

1. Read John 8:31-32. What does it mean to be set free by the truth?

2. How do you go about discovering the depths of this truth that brings freedom? In other words, how can you go beyond rules and traditions to discover the truths of who God is and how He desires us to live?

APPLY IT...

3. Martin Luther believed so deeply in living by the truth of God's Word that he was willing to face the threats of imprisonment and death. How willing are you to live by and for the truth of God's Word?

4. Martin was concerned that the religious traditions the church held to were actually hindering believers from understanding salvations and becoming all that Christ had called them to be. Are there religious traditions in your life that may be keeping you from living out all that Christ intends for you?

TAKE ACTION!

What are some important issues in our society today that require Christians to stand for truth, even if their views are unpopular? Choose one issue that strikes a chord in you, and identify one way that you can stand for truth on that issue, under the authority of God's Word.

WATCHMAN NEE

1903-1972

DECLARATION 9
IT'S MY TURN TO
SHARE IN CHRIST'S SUFFERINGS

KNOWN THROUGHOUT HIS SCHOOL YEARS as a bright and talented student, Watchman Nee had plenty of big dreams for future success. What he didn't know was that by following Christ, his life would prove successful in a very different way. Watchman's leadership led to the rapid growth of the church in China—and his faithfulness to God in the midst of great suffering provided an inspiring example to believers worldwide.

Nee Shu-tsu (his given name at birth) had heard the Gospel since he was a small boy, but at age seventeen, he could ignore God no longer—and he realized that accepting Jesus would unquestionably mean serving him.

"At that time I was afraid of being saved, for I knew that once I was saved I must serve the Lord," Watchman said. "…It was impossible for me to set aside the Lord's calling and to desire only salvation." He couldn't simply receive Jesus as Savior; he knew that Jesus must also be Lord of his life. That night, he accepted Christ as his Lord and was immediately called to be a preacher.

The Chinese have a custom of choosing a new name after a significant milestone in their lives, so after his conversion, Nee Shu-tsu selected the name Nee To-sheng: "Watchman Nee" in English. He saw himself as the watchman who would sound the warning and deliver the Gospel to the people of China.

Watchman began to share his faith with his Trinity College classmates and hold prayer meetings with new believers, and the Gospel soon spread beyond the college. Revival came to the city of Foochow—countless young people came to Christ, and their ministry branched out to the surrounding cities and villages. Watchman's vision was for local churches to emerge across China.

For the sake of God's work, Watchman faced poverty, sickness, opposition from denominations, dissension among believers in the local churches, and ultimately, government persecution. But even though he was constantly under attack, he submitted to the sovereignty of God. He saw his suffering not only as a "thorn in the flesh," like the apostle Paul, but also as a means for growth. "You must allow God to give you time to suffer beyond measure," he said. "Then your capacity will be enlarged."

And God certainly used suffering to expand Watchman's influence. For example, when Watchman contracted tuberculosis, he had to stop traveling and preaching for a time—so he began writing instead, and his works contributed to the growth of countless believers.

Watchman relocated his ministry to Shanghai and worked to build local churches there. As his ministry flourished, he suffered at the hands of false witnesses who spread rumors about him and tried to discredit his ministry. After he married Charity Chang, her aunt (who disapproved of the marriage) spread evil stories about him. He was then rejected by a group of English brothers who had once befriended him and supported his ministry. Yet throughout these persecutions, Watchman refused to defend himself. He stood firm in the Lord, believing that he had been crucified with Christ and that God and His truth would prevail.

The church in Shanghai grew rapidly, and Watchman developed a plan for Shanghai families to spread out to different areas and take the Gospel with them, planting churches all over China. When the Communist Party began to notice Watchman's growing ministry, many of his co-workers urged him to stay in Hong Kong rather than return to mainland China because of the danger. He responded, "If a mother discovered that her house was on fire, and she herself was outside the house doing the laundry, what would she do? Although she realized the danger, would she not rush into the house? Although I know that my return is fraught with dangers, I know that many brothers and sisters are still inside. How can I not return?"

The Communist army soon entered Shanghai and closed all churches, and in the spring of 1952, they arrested Watchman because of his faith in Christ and his leadership of churches that were not under Communist authority. A 2,296-page indictment against him contained all sorts of false accusations, ranging from espionage and counterrevolutionary activities to immorality and financial mishandlings. He appeared before his accusers for twelve straight days, and ultimately he was sentenced to prison at age fifty. He would never again be free.

Though some details are clear, no one knows the extent of the suffering Watchman endured over the next twenty years. Guards confiscated his Bible, and he was allowed no contact or communication with the outside world. His days consisted of eight hours of hard labor, eight hours alone in a dark cell, and eight hours of "re-education," during which the Communists tried to brainwash him through long periods of interrogation and lectures. But Watchman stood fast. He passed the time by reciting Scripture and singing songs he wrote from Bible verses. He witnessed to those around him, and one of the prison guards even became a Christian. Meanwhile, his writings inspired a revival among Chinese students.

Watchman died in confinement in a prison cell on May 30, 1972. Under his pillow, he left a piece of paper on which he had written, "Christ is the Son of God who died for the redemption of sinners and resurrected after three days. This is the greatest truth in the universe. I die because of my belief in Christ. Watchman Nee."

Right up to his death, Watchman Nee testified to the truth he spent his life promoting and defending. And his martyrdom, combined with all the other persecution in China, has produced phenomenal growth among Chinese believers by inspiring them to stand firm and suffer for Christ.

"NOTHING HURTS SO MUCH AS DISSATISFACTION WITH OUR CIRCUMSTANCES. WE ALL START FROM REST, BUT THERE IS ANOTHER REST WHICH WE DISCOVER WHEN WE LEARN FROM JESUS HOW TO SAY, 'I THANK YOU, FATHER, FOR IT SEEMED GOOD TO THEE.' GOD KNOWS WHAT HE IS DOING AND THERE IS NOTHING ACCIDENTAL IN THE LIFE OF THE BELIEVER. NOTHING BUT GOOD CAN COME TO THOSE WHO ARE WHOLLY HIS."

SIGNIFICANT CONTRIBUTION

Watchman Nee used preaching, teaching, traveling, correspondence with people, conferences, training, and writing to spread the Gospel. And his suffering fueled the growth of the Chinese church. At the time of his arrest, four hundred local churches had been raised up in China as a result of his ministry, as well as more than thirty churches in other countries in Southeast Asia. Today, there are more than 2,300 churches worldwide because of Watchman's faithful witness for Christ.

FOCUS SCRIPTURE

"Dear friends, do not be surprised at the painful trial you are suffering, as though something strange were happening to you. But rejoice that you participate in the sufferings of Christ, so that you may be overjoyed when his glory is revealed." (1 Peter 4:12-13)

THINK ABOUT IT...

1. Read 1 Peter 4:12-16. Why shouldn't you be surprised if you suffer from painful trials?

2. Watchman said, "If you cannot stand the trials of the cross, you cannot become a useful instrument. It is only the spirit of the lamb that God takes delight in: the gentleness, the humility, and the peace." What do you think he meant? How can trials make you a more useful instrument and "enlarge your capacity," as Watchman said they did for him?

APPLY IT...

3. Many times, Watchman was falsely accused of evil and his enemies spread rumors about him. Yet he never tried to defend himself. Have you ever been falsely accused or been the subject of rumors? What do you think is a godly response?

4. American Christians today rarely suffer the kind of persecution that Watchman Nee faced. But what other kinds of suffering or persecution might you or others face? How can you stand firm in the midst of such suffering?

5. Even though he suffered greatly for his faith, Watchman said, "Nothing but good can come to those who are wholly [God's]." How do you think he could maintain such a perspective? How can you view the bad things that happen to you from this perspective?

TAKE ACTION!

Though we may not be persecuted in America today, Hebrews 13:3 says, "Remember those in prison as if you were their fellow prisoners, and those who are mistreated as if you yourselves were suffering." Take some time to check out the website for The Voice of the Martyrs at www.persecution.com, where you can read about persecuted Christians today. Write a letter to an imprisoned believer, commit to praying for your suffering brothers and sisters overseas, make a donation to help the persecuted church, or sign up to receive regular updates from The Voice of the Martyrs.

WILLIAM WILBERFORCE

1759-1833

DECLARATION 10
IT'S MY TURN TO RUN THE
RACE OF FAITH WITH PERSEVERANCE

WILLIAM WILBERFORCE went from a young politician too concerned about others' opinions to follow Christ to a revered and respected champion of the abolition movement in England. His crusade to end slavery wasn't easy, but his years of hard work and his refusal to give up finally paid off when it resulted in the freedom of slaves throughout the British Empire.

During his first years in Parliament, William didn't care about much except recognition—his charm and eloquence made him an admired politician. He wasn't following Christ and had ambitions only for his own advancement and success. Though he had grown up with plenty of exposure to the Gospel, he said he was "afraid to surrender to Christ for fear of what others might say." Then he came to what he called a crisis of his soul. "I am afraid of turning my back on Christ," he said. "But I also fear losing face and prestige. If my constituents were to hear that I embraced...religion, my career would be over."

William spent time wrestling with those fears, and over a period of time during 1785 and 1786, inward reflection led to salvation. Initially, William considered leaving politics to enter vocational ministry, but John Newton discouraged the idea. "Imagine what [God] can do through a gifted member of Parliament," he said. "There's nothing in the Bible that says you cannot be both a Christian and a statesman."

After his conversion, William was very vocal in Parliament about his new faith, which at first brought ridicule from his colleagues—but eventually, they began to respect him for his passionate beliefs. And William became an activist. He found a new sense of purpose, saying, "God Almighty has set before me two great objects, the suppression of the Slave Trade and the reformation of manners."

His first focus was to develop a "Society for the Suppression of Vice," which would enforce laws against such things as Sabbath-breaking, drunkenness, lotteries, blasphemy, and unlicensed entertainment. This idea didn't go very far, and in fact, William met with much scorn and opposition. Still he persevered. In 1793, when the East India Company's charter was up for renewal, William proposed resolutions that would allow missionaries to travel to India—but he lost again.

Soon, however, he narrowed his focus and concentrated on slavery. Throughout the 1700s, the slave trade in the British Empire had been viewed as a necessary evil. By 1787, several abolitionists formed a Committee for the Abolition of the Slave Trade, but they needed a voice in Parliament. William was the perfect candidate—influential and independent, an eloquent speaker with a quick mind.

"So enormous, so dreadful, so irremediable did the trade's wickedness appear that my own mind was completely made up for abolition," he said. "Let the consequences be what they would: I from this time determined that I would never rest until I had effected its abolition."

The committee took action, and in 1789, William gave a three-hour speech on abolition, describing the capture of slaves and the ocean passage they faced. He then introduced the first motion to abolish slave trade. Debate on the bill began in 1791, but his opponents prevailed and the bill was rejected.

The next year, William tried again, pleading for the slaves in a speech: "Africa! Africa!" he cried. "Your sufferings have been the theme that has arrested and engages my heart—your sufferings no tongue can express; no language impart." By 1792, he had become such a prominent opponent of slavery that captains in the West Indies threatened his life. But John Wesley wrote to encourage him: "Unless God has raised you up for this very thing, you will be worn out by the opposition of men and devils, but if God be for you who can be against you? ...Oh be not weary of well-doing. Go on in the name of God, and in the power of his might, till even American slavery, the vilest that ever saw the sun, shall vanish away before it."

Over the next seventeen years, abolitionists took their arguments to the public, seeking to convince the people of their cause and obtain petitions. They tried various methods of lessening the horror of the slave trade, such as advocating more humane treatment or regulating the trade, but without much success. Abolition was blocked in Parliament by vested interests, filibusters, bigotry, international politics, and slave unrest. And abolitionists were heavily persecuted by pro-slavery activists.

Still William did not give up the fight. And in 1807, the House of Commons voted by a huge majority to abolish the slave trade in the British Empire. It was a day of triumph—but William's work was not done. Though trading new slaves was now illegal, owning slaves was not. William and his colleagues began working to ensure enforcement of the slave trade law and to eventually abolish slavery altogether. But it would be a long fight.

By 1817, William had set his sights on the emancipation of all slaves, but he was old and sick, leaving him unable to lead a fight in Parliament. Finally in 1833, he spoke in Parliament against slavery. And after forty-five years as a politician, William Wilberforce saw his vision fulfilled. On July 26, 1833, just four days before his death, Parliament passed the Bill for the Abolition of Slavery in all British territories.

> "MY WALK IS A PUBLIC ONE. MY BUSINESS IS IN THE WORLD, AND I MUST MIX IN THE ASSEMBLIES OF MEN OR QUIT THE POST WHICH PROVIDENCE SEEMS TO HAVE ASSIGNED ME."

SIGNIFICANT CONTRIBUTION

William Wilberforce led the long and arduous crusade to end the practice of slavery in the British Empire, which paved the way for the end of slavery in America. His perseverance in the face of criticism and ridicule and his refusal to back down made him a hero at last. Because of William's work in the field where God had placed him—politics—abolitionists had a powerful voice and slaves could finally be freed.

FOCUS SCRIPTURE

"Let us not become weary in doing good, for at the proper time we will reap a harvest if we do not give up."(Galatians 6:9)

THINK ABOUT IT...

1. Read Galatians 6:9. Why do we often become weary in doing good—what makes us want to give up?

2. How do you think William was able to persevere through so many long years of what might have seemed like a hopeless battle?

APPLY IT...

3. Sometimes we, like William, may face situations when it seems like our dreams are hopeless—that even though our desires are noble and right, they aren't becoming reality. When it looks like your godly hopes and desires may not be fulfilled, how do you respond?

4. When people are critical of your convictions, what kind of impact does that have on you? Do you turn to God for strength to help you persevere, or do you succumb to the pressures of others?

TAKE ACTION!

What is one conviction that you know you have compromised on because it was too hard or too lonely or too radical? Find one person to confess this to and ask them to pray with you and support you as you strive to live out this conviction and persevere through opposition.

SUSANNA WESLEY

1669-1742

DECLARATION 11
IT'S MY TURN TO ADVANCE THE KINGDOM IN THE ROLE UNIQUELY DESIGNED FOR ME BY GOD

SUSANNA WESLEY HAD NINETEEN KIDS in just twenty-one years, and though nine of them died in infancy, she devoted her life to raising the other ten to become strong men and women of God. She proved that a person doesn't have to be famous or have a publicly prominent ministry in order to advance the Kingdom.

Susanna's family ministry began with her marriage to the Reverend Samuel Wesley. She had grown up with a comfortable lifestyle in London, but she soon moved to the country with her husband, and he began pastoring a church where the people were considered backwards. Samuel was not well suited to country life or to managing business affairs and family finances—so Susanna took over those things. In doing so, she gracefully honored and supported her husband without making him look incompetent or foolish. Samuel expressed his admiration for his wife in a poem, which included these lines: "She graced my humble roof, and blest my life, / Blest me by a far greater name than wife."

At age twenty-one, she had her first son, and her life soon became consumed with the care and upbringing of her children. Susanna's purpose was clear: "There is nothing I now desire to live for but to do some small service to my children," she said, "that as I have brought them into the world, I may, if it please God, be an instrument of doing good to their souls." Though the Wesley family had lots of kids and little money, they were known as a loving, bright, and disciplined family.

Susanna undoubtedly had to make sacrifices for the sake of her children, but to her, the ultimate goal was worth any cost. She wrote, "No one can, without renouncing the world, in the most literal sense, observe my method; and there are few, if any, that would entirely devote above twenty years of the prime of life in hopes to save the souls of their children, which they think may be saved without so much ado; for that was my principal intention, however unskillfully and unsuccessfully managed."

Because the Wesley family could not afford private tutors (the typical method of education in that day), Susanna homeschooled her children. Most women of her time were not educated, but her father had taught her, and she in turn cultivated a love of learning in her kids. The family had little money for textbooks, so Susanna taught from library books, the Bible, and material she wrote herself. She even wrote a manual about the religious instruction of her children, in which she explained religion, drafted a commentary on the Ten Commandments, and outlined the primary elements of Christianity based on the Apostles' Creed.

Susanna was strict with her children, but she was also very patient. One day, as her husband observed her teaching, he watched her repeat the same lesson to a child over and over. Finally he grew impatient and exclaimed, "I wonder at your patience! You have told that child twenty times the same thing." She answered, "If I had satisfied myself by mentioning it only nineteen times, I should have lost all my labor. It was the twentieth time that crowned it."

Susanna's role as a mother went beyond educator and disciplinarian—she was also a mentor and friend. For years, she managed to schedule weekly individual time with every child. Once her children left home, she faithfully corresponded with them through frequent letters, and the writings of her sons John and Charles show the value they placed on her counsel and guidance.

Although caring for her children consumed most of her time, Susanna was deeply devoted to God and placed a high priority on personal holiness. She made it her rule "never to spend more time in any matter of mere recreation in one day than spent in private religious duties." Susanna faithfully spent an hour in solitude with the Lord in the early morning and in the evening each day, not allowing anything to interfere with those times. Yet she found communion with God not only in prayer or study, but in the everyday tasks set before her as a wife and mother. She wrote, "Religion is not to be confined to the church or closet, nor exercised only in prayer and meditation, but everywhere I am in His presence."

Susanna's ministry and responsibilities were not limited to her husband and children. She also oversaw the church while her husband was in London for conferences, directed the farming of their land, and managed family finances. She took on roles of spiritual leadership as well. When her husband was in London, she held evening worship services for her family in the kitchen. Susanna and the children would sing psalms, read prayers, and listen to a short sermon from Samuel's library. Soon the servants started coming, then relatives, friends, and neighbors. Eventually, more than two hundred people attended!

But her greatest contribution to the world was her children, whom she raised with wisdom and unselfish love. That devotion is reflected in the success of their lives, particularly John and Charles. John was very close to his mother—he called her the greatest influence in his life. The self-examination and methodical practice of holiness he saw in her life became hallmarks of the Methodist movement that John started.

"I AM CONTENT TO FILL A LITTLE SPACE IF GOD BE GLORIFIED."

Susanna's final request as she lay dying was a simple one: "Children," she said, "as soon as I am released, sing a psalm of praise to God." And they did. To the end of her life, Susanna Wesley exemplified the words of Proverbs 31:28: "Her children arise and call her blessed; her husband also, and he praises her." She stands as an example of the profound impact a woman can have in building the Kingdom through a ministry that starts with home and family.

SIGNIFICANT CONTRIBUTION

Susanna Wesley raised nine children in an atmosphere of love, discipline and godliness. She devoted her life to the intellectual and spiritual education of her children, seeking to produce a generation of her family who would follow Christ devotedly. Her son Charles is considered one of the greatest hymn writers of all time, and her son John founded the Methodist church. Susanna has also been called the "Mother of Methodism" because John modeled much of the Methodist movement after practices he learned from her.

FOCUS SCRIPTURE

"For we are God's workmanship, created in Christ Jesus to do good works, which God prepared in advance for us to do." (Ephesians 2:10)

THINK ABOUT IT...

1. Read Ephesians 2:10. How does it affect your understanding of your life and your importance to know that God has prepared good works in advance for you to do?

2. How do you think Susanna would be viewed in today's society— admired and respected, or looked down upon? Why?

3. In Hebrews 11, people are celebrated not as much for what they accomplish, but for their faithfulness. How can we as Christians miss the significance of people in Hebrews 11 or other faithful believers like Susanna Wesley through our focus on results and our culture's definitions of success?

APPLY IT...

4. Who has been the most influential person in your life? Was it a famous person, or someone you knew well? How has this person shaped you?

5. Take a few moments to brainstorm what "unique and distinct ministry" might look like in your life. What interests has God given you? Burdens or passions? Talents? Skills? Training or experiences?

6. Susanna recognized the purpose for which God had made her and the circumstances in which He had placed her and did her best to serve Him where she was. Honestly assess your life and attitudes: Do you look for ways God can use you right where you are, in the ordinary parts of life, or are you always looking past the mundane to find a celebrated ministry outlet?

TAKE ACTION!

If you haven't already done so, consider developing a "life mission statement"—a clear, concise, broad, and inspiring statement of your life purpose and how you believe God is calling you to advance His Kingdom.
(Check out www.keepgrowinginc.com for guidance and resources to help you with this.)

ERIC LIDDELL

1902-1945

DECLARATION 12
IT'S MY TURN TO USE MY GOD-GIVEN GIFTS FOR HIS GLORY

BORN IN CHINA as the son of scottish missionaries, Eric Liddell knew from the time he was a kid that he wanted to follow in his father's mission work. But Eric also excelled at sports. He won many races when he was young, and although he originally intended to abandon sports once he began college in Scotland, a persuasive friend talked him into participating on the track team. Soon he saw that before leaving for China, he had an opportunity to glorify God with his athletic talents.

The more Eric ran, the more his fame grew. But he quickly became embarrassed by all the publicity. He preferred instead to think of the attention and praise as for his team, his university, or his country.

By the time Eric Liddell reached the 1924 Olympics in Paris, he was favored to win the 100-meter dash. But to everyone's astonishment, he withdrew from the race once the schedule was released. It would be held on a Sunday, and Eric felt strongly that Sunday should be set apart for rest and worship. Some people wondered why he couldn't just make an exception; others even suggested changing the day of the race! But although he was disappointed, he didn't hesitate—he simply withdrew from the races that were to be held that day.

Eric had been Scotland's best hope for a medal, so the officials decided to put him in a different event. Although the longer races weren't his strength, he entered the 400-meter run. And God blessed Eric that day for his commitment to honor God. No one thought a 100-meter sprinter could succeed at the 400-meter race—but he shocked the world by winning a gold medal and setting a new world record!

For Eric, running wasn't just about fun or exercise—it was a way to bring glory to God with the talents he had been given. When his sister tried to persuade him to leave sooner for China, he said, "I believe that God made me for a purpose for China. But He also made me fast, and when I run, I feel His pleasure. To give it up would be to hold Him in contempt. You were right, it's not just fun. To win is to honor Him."

But Eric also knew that it wasn't all about winning. When people honored him after his Olympic victory, he was quick to remember an injured teammate, who had previously been Scotland's best hope for the 400-meter race. "In the dust of defeat as well as the laurels of victory, there is a glory to be found if one has done his best," he said.

In addition to simply running for God's glory, Eric was eventually able to use his fame to draw people to the Lord. For years he didn't speak openly about his faith—he just lived it out. Then the leaders of a local evangelistic crusade asked him to come and speak. They knew the famous athlete would draw big crowds. That experience sparked Eric's interest, and soon he began going to crusades and sharing his faith with the crowds.

Beyond all the fame and Olympic glory, a deeper passion burned within Eric. Before long, he knew the time had come to pursue the missionary calling God had placed on his life. Within weeks after returning from Paris, he announced that he had been offered a teaching position at a university in Tientsin, China. He explained that he would be fully devoting himself to preparing for missionary life.

Eric asked for and received a one-year deferment on his teaching assignment in China, using the time to study theology and to travel and speak. He knew that God had given him a unique platform for influence, and he was determined to use it to exalt the name of Christ. He spoke in theaters, churches, dance halls, social clubs—wherever an audience could gather, he was happy to share his story and his Lord. And scores of people came to Christ in those 1924-25 crusades.

When the day came for him to leave for China, a huge crowd gathered at the train station to see him off, and in reverence and respect for his faith, the crowd sang one of his favorite hymns. At age twenty-three, just one year after he had captured the attention of the world and had become an Olympic champion, Eric headed to China, where he would spend the rest of his life sharing God's love and truth with the Chinese people.

Eric's impact in China was just as powerful as his influence back home. When his students at the Anglo-Chinese College found out that their teacher was famous in his home country, they couldn't understand why he would abandon all that success and fame in order to come to China. This led them to believe that Eric's God must be special. He also continued running in China, and when the students saw him run, they couldn't believe anyone could be so fast—and that strengthened their belief in his God.

Eric Liddell died of a brain tumor while being held captive in a Japanese internment camp during World War II. His life was documented in the Academy Award-winning film Chariots of Fire. He had used his God-given talents in a way that surely brought a smile to the heart of his Creator—and when his life was over, he could say with confidence, like the apostle Paul, "I have fought the good fight, I have finished the race, I have kept the faith" (2 Timothy 4:7).

> *"I BELIEVE THAT GOD MADE ME FOR A PURPOSE—FOR CHINA. BUT HE ALSO MADE ME FAST, AND WHEN I RUN, I FEEL HIS PLEASURE. TO GIVE IT UP WOULD BE TO HOLD HIM IN CONTEMPT."*

SIGNIFICANT CONTRIBUTION

As an Olympic athlete, Eric Liddell used his talents for the glory of God. He sought to honor the Lord with his fame and success by using it as a platform to draw people to Christ. And he laid aside that fame and fortune in order to pursue God's call by serving as a missionary in China. His life demonstrates that a laborer's activities don't have to be overtly "spiritual" in order to be pleasing to God and bring glory to Him.

FOCUS SCRIPTURE

"And whatever you do, whether in word or deed, do it all in the name of the Lord Jesus, giving thanks to God the Father through him." (Colossians 3:17)

THINK ABOUT IT...

1. Read Colossians 3:17. Often many Christians see only ministry work as being truly valuable service for God. Is this in line with a Biblical understanding of God's heart and His purpose for the world? Why or why not?

2. When Eric made the commitment to rest on Sundays, he probably never imagined that the decision would cost him an Olympic gold medal. But he followed through on his commitment and stuck to his beliefs even when it was hard. Do you think God would have been glorified in the same way if Eric had changed his mind and run on Sunday in spite of his convictions? Why or why not?

APPLY IT...

3. Have you ever had to make a decision like the one Eric made, giving up something that you wanted in order to do what you knew was right? Explain. What enables you to keep your commitments when an opportunity comes up that seems better?

4. Eric refused to run in the Olympics on Sunday because he was committed to setting aside time for God. What benefits can you think of from setting one day apart to honor the Lord? What could you choose not to do on that day (whether Sunday or another day)? What could you do instead?

5. Eric saw his ability to run as useful for advancing God's Kingdom. What talents, skills or gifts do you have, apart from traditional ministry skills and opportunities, that God could use to further his Kingdom? List some ideas about how you could use these to glorify God.

TAKE ACTION!

The parable of the talents in Matthew 25:14-30 talks about developing and using what God has given us to serve Him. The focus is not on what gifts you have, or how many, but on whether you're using what you have to the best of your ability. Identify one of your primary talents or skills that you could develop more in the coming weeks and months, and find at least one practical way to sharpen it so that you're better prepared to use it for God's glory.

IT'S MY TURN ›› FOLLOW IN THE FOOTSTEPS OF CHRISTIANS WHO IMPACTED THEIR WORLD

DWIGHT L. MOODY

1837-1899

DECLARATION 13
IT'S MY TURN TO SHARE THE GOSPEL

IN 1855, DWIGHT MOODY WAS AN AMBITIOUS TEENAGER who had no higher goal than to earn a fortune of $100,000. But the boldness of a Sunday School teacher led Dwight to shift his focus, and he devoted the rest of his life to the spread of the Gospel, influencing millions to receive Christ.

After reaching only a fifth-grade education, Dwight moved to Boston at age seventeen to work in his uncle's shoe store. His uncle set just one condition: Dwight had to attend church. He went to a Sunday School class taught by Ed Kimball, and one day, Ed felt a tugging in his heart to share his faith with his young student. At first he hesitated, but he finally mustered the courage to enter the shoe store where Dwight worked. Ed found him in the back room stocking shoes, and he shared the Gospel with him.

Dwight never forgot the bold actions of this ordinary man who led him to a relationship with Christ. It compelled him to be bold in sharing his own faith with others. After all, he reasoned, if an ordinary man like Ed Kimball could be used in such ways to build God's Kingdom, so could he.

After his conversion, he moved to Chicago to work toward the fortune he hoped to attain—but he soon began to realize that perhaps his life could be spent pursuing more worthwhile goals. Dwight established a Sunday School in the Chicago slums and ministered to many children in the city, gathering them from the streets and docks and telling them Bible stories.

Despite the fact that he failed to pass requirements for ordination as a pastor, Dwight left the business world completely in 1861 in order to concentrate on social work and evangelism. His Sunday School in the slums grew into a full-fledged church, and Dwight was tireless in his efforts to reach the people around him for Christ. He distributed tracts and held prayer meetings at noon each day, and he helped to evangelize the Union troops during the Civil War. His methods were simple, but effective: "If you can really make a man believe you love him, you have won him," he said.

One night in 1871, Dwight was preaching on how God desired everyone to repent and be saved. Since it was a series of meetings on the subject, he told the people to return the next evening for an opportunity to respond to the Gospel message. But that opportunity never came for many in the audience. That night, the Great Chicago Fire broke out, and hundreds lost their lives—including many who had heard Dwight preach that evening. He was devastated, and he determined that he would never again miss a chance to compel people to respond immediately to the message of Christ.

Shortly after the fire, which destroyed not only his church, but also his home and the YMCA where he ministered, Dwight traveled to New York to raise money for rebuilding the church. While he was there, he had another experience that profoundly affected his ministry. As he walked down Wall Street, he felt "a presence and power" unlike anything he'd ever experienced. The encounter was so powerful that he cried out, "Hold Lord, it is enough!" Dwight received a new sense of purpose and empowerment from the Spirit of God and a fresh vision for his ministry. He realized that his focus had to be on preaching the Gospel, not just on social work, and he gave himself to the cause of the "evangelization of the world in this generation."

When he returned to Chicago, Dwight noticed the difference in his ministry. He said that his "sermons were no different, but now hundreds were being saved." At that point, he set a goal for himself. He determined that he was going to win someone for Christ every day for the rest of his life, God willing. He wrote the commitment down in his journal and said he kept it "even if he didn't get any sleep at night."

He also began traveling extensively with a gospel singer named Ira Sankey. Together, they developed hugely popular revivals and crusades in America and Great Britain. They pioneered several crusade evangelism techniques that are still used today, including canvassing houses, renting a large building, using a gospel singer, getting all local churches to cooperate, and providing an "inquiry room" for those who want to repent.

In the course of his ministry, Dwight established three Christian schools, a publishing business, a Christian conference, and a Bible institute. He was also instrumental in inspiring preachers to win souls through revival. And he didn't let up at the end—just one month before he died, he was still preaching six sermons a day!

It is said that Dwight Moody traveled a million miles, preached to one hundred million people, and won a million souls to Christ. He chose to center his ministry in Chicago and focus primarily on the worst sections of the city, believing that no one else would care to reach those people. Though an ordinary man in many ways, he was compelled by an intense passion for lost souls, and he left a legacy of countless new believers behind him.

> *"IF THIS WORLD IS GOING TO BE REACHED, I AM CONVINCED THAT IT MUST BE DONE BY MEN AND WOMEN OF AVERAGE TALENT. AFTER ALL, THERE ARE COMPARATIVELY FEW PEOPLE IN THIS WORLD WHO HAVE GREAT TALENTS."*

SIGNIFICANT CONTRIBUTION

In spite of his lack of formal training, Dwight Moody did more to reach his generation for Christ than any other layman. Through popularizing the Sunday School and pioneering many aspects of crusade evangelism, he won countless souls for Christ. He also founded Moody Bible Institute, one of the first and most well-known Bible colleges in the nation.

FOCUS SCRIPTURE

"Therefore go and make disciples of all nations, baptizing them in the name of the Father and of the Son and of the Holy Spirit, and teaching them to obey everything I have commanded you. And surely I am with you always, to the very end of the age." (Matthew 28:19-20)

THINK ABOUT IT...

1. Read Matthew 28:19-20. This passage is commonly referred to as the "Great Commission." Though it seems like just one command, it includes two things that we are called to do and one thing that God promises to do. Identify these different parts. What about this passage encourages you or excites you? What about this passage makes you afraid or uneasy?

2. Dwight Moody once said, "Before my conversion I worked toward the cross, but since then I have worked from the cross; then I worked to be saved, now I work because I am saved." What do you think he meant by this?

APPLY IT...

3. Do you have a hard time sharing your faith with others? If so, what are some of the obstacles that hold you back? How can you work to overcome these?

4. Evangelism isn't just about walking up to a stranger on the street and sharing the "Romans Roads" or some other catchy technique or tract. While this can be valuable at times, for many people it's not very effective. A different perspective on sharing the Gospel is "relational evangelism." What is relational evangelism? What are some "outside the box" ways that you could share Christ's love and truth in your relationships with lost people?

TAKE ACTION!

List five people in your sphere of influence who do not know Christ. Then make a commitment to pray for each of these people daily and whenever else the Holy Spirit brings them to your mind. Put the list somewhere that you will see it often and be reminded to pray for their salvation—and believe that "you will receive whatever you ask for in prayer" (Matthew 21:22). But remember that you may be part of God's answer to your prayer—so ask Him to give you boldness to share your faith with them as well.

WILLIAM CAREY

1761-1834

DECLARATION 14
IT'S MY TURN TO BLESS THE NATIONS

AS A YOUNG MAN, William Carey studied geography and collected information on a homemade globe, reflecting on the neglected countries of the world and praying that God would make a way for him to help the "heathen nations" living in darkness. A book called Journal of Captain Cook's Last Voyage, which chronicled the adventures of a British sea captain in the South Pacific, had stirred his mind toward missions, and his sister later noted that she never heard William pray without including the heathen nations. To him, they weren't just statistics—they were people who needed to hear the good news about Jesus Christ. The constant theme of his life was the "infinite worth of a single soul."

William had no qualifications to be a missionary except an undeniable conviction that God had called him to "the conversion of the heathens." He was ordained as a preacher at age twenty-five, and although he poured himself into local church ministry, his dreams of reaching out to faraway lands never left him. As a minister, he was invited to join a church association in Northampton, England. At a meeting of this association in 1786, the group was asked to propose a discussion topic, and after a silence, William suggested they discuss "the duty of Christians to attempt the spread of the Gospel among heathen nations."

His suggestion was harshly rebuked by the group's chairman, Mr. Ryland. "Young man, sit down!" Ryland exclaimed. "When God pleases to convert the heathen He will do it without your aid or mine." William was called a "miserable enthusiast." He was publicly humiliated and received no support from his peers, who saw his ideas as crazy and farfetched. Clearly, he had plenty of reasons to give up—but he didn't abandon the mission God had placed in his heart.

Two years later, William met a man named Thomas Potts, who implored him to put his ideas in print. Thomas even contributed ten pounds toward the printing of a pamphlet exhorting Christians to accept responsibility for the evangelization of the heathen. So William accepted the challenge and drew upon his eight years of research to write out his thoughts about missions. He didn't start from scratch, but built on the work of other pioneering missionaries, such as John Eliot and David Brainerd (missionaries to Native Americans) and Count Nicholas von Zinzendorf.

The result was an eighty-seven page booklet titled An Enquiry Into the Obligations of Christians to Use Means For the Conversion of the Heathens. The booklet's five chapters covered the Great Commission; historical precedents; geography and spiritual and cultural information about the world; obstacles; and the Christian's duty to missions. He also laid out a three-point plan for evangelizing the heathen: pray, plan, and give.

The influence of his Enquiry opened the door for him to speak before the Northamptonshire Baptist Association, a gathering of several local churches for mutual support and service. In 1792, he preached before the association from Isaiah 54:2-3—"Enlarge the place of thy tent...thy seed shall inherit the Gentiles" (KJV). He summed up his fiery challenge to reach out to heathen nations with these words: "Expect great things. Attempt great things."

On October 2, 1792, the Northamptonshire Association adopted a resolution creating the first Protestant mission agency. The London Missionary Society was then organized in 1795. William himself was torn over whether to go overseas—he felt compelled to respond to the call to missions, yet the church where he pastored was thriving, and his family objected. And once he finally decided to go, he met with many obstacles, including the fact that missionaries couldn't get licenses from the East India Company for permission to go. But he finally made it to India, where he opened schools and promoted literacy and education. His strategy in India had three parts: preach the gospel, translate the Bible, and open schools. And the first Hindu believer was baptized in 1800.

He soon discovered that he had a gift for learning languages, and he worked over seven years to complete the first Bengali New Testament. By 1837, he and his co-workers had translated the Bible into forty languages and dialects! William was personally responsible for six total translations and parts of twenty-nine others.

William also dreamed of missionary families living in close community and modeling the Gospel to the nationals, and he envisioned cooperation between all worldwide missions efforts. He hoped that there would someday be an international gathering of all denominations for the advance of missions. (His dream was realized one hundred years later at the International Mission Conference in Edinburgh, Scotland, in 1910.) "[Let us work] with indefatigable industry, till we can't find a soul that's destitute of Christ in all the world," he said.

William Carey spent more than forty years as a missionary in India. Yet on his deathbed, he said, "When I am gone, say nothing about Dr. Carey. Speak about Dr. Carey's Savior."

> *"WHAT IS THERE IN ALL THIS WORLD WORTH LIVING FOR, BUT THE PRESENCE AND SERVICE OF GOD? I FEEL A BURNING DESIRE THAT ALL THE WORLD MAY KNOW THIS GOD, AND SERVE HIM."*

SIGNIFICANT CONTRIBUTION

Because of his public stand for missions among pastors in England and his pioneer missionary efforts in India, William Carey is known as the Father of Modern Missions. His recognition of the need for contextualization and respect for the national culture provided a lasting model for missionaries today.

FOCUS SCRIPTURE

"Declare his glory among the nations, his marvelous deeds among all peoples."
(Psalm 96:3)

THINK ABOUT IT...

1. Read Psalm 96. What does it mean to declare God's glory among the nations?

2. William Carey was a pioneering missionary especially because of his respect for the national culture. When the first person was converted in India, William said that the new believer "became a Christian, not a European." What do you think he meant by this? What are the characteristics that should be true of all Christians, regardless of culture? (Back your answers up with Scripture.)

APPLY IT...

3. On a scale of 1-10, assess your level of interest and concern for the spread of the Gospel among the "heathen nations"—people of the world who have not yet heard the good news of Christ. Why do you think you feel the way you do? How can you increase your passion for seeing the Gospel preached throughout the world?

4. Often what you pray for, where you spend your money, and how you invest your time can indicate your priorities. In your own life, what do these things say about your heart for the unreached world?

5. Revelation 7:9 describes "a great multitude...from every nation, tribe, people and language, standing before the throne." Why do you think the Bible places such an emphasis on the diversity of people in heaven? What can you learn about God's character from seeing His desire for all nations to know and be saved?

TAKE ACTION!

As a young man, William Carey made a map of the world and hung it on the wall over his cobbler's bench, so that he could pray for each country while he worked. Use the Internet or a library to find information about countries where Christians are striving to advance the Gospel. Select a few nations and pray for the advancement of the Gospel there. But William also wrote, "We must plan and plod as well as pray." Try to find one specific way you can participate in the advancement of the Gospel in these countries.

DAWSON TROTMAN

1906-1956

DECLARATION 15
IT'S MY TURN TO
REPRODUCE OTHER LABORERS

DAWSON TROTMAN LIVED THE FAST LIFE in high school—he spent his time gambling, drinking, stealing, and stunt driving. Though he deceived himself into believing he was a Christian, it wasn't until age twenty that he became a true follower of Christ. God spoke to him through Scriptures he had memorized for a contest, and he suddenly realized his need for a real relationship with God. He began living boldly and witnessing to his friends, and his life purpose became clear: He wanted to know Christ, and he wanted to make Christ known to every person he encountered.

Soon Dawson joined a Fishermen Club, a group that emphasized evangelism and studying the Bible. He sought to impact every person he met for Christ, often praying, "Lord, we're just reporting for duty. We don't know who we'll meet today or what their need will be, but give us the right word for them."

Before long, though, Dawson began to see the difference between winning souls and making disciples—between believers and laborers. He shifted his focus, concentrating not just on getting people to make one-time decisions for Christ, but on building disciples God could trust. No longer could he evangelize without discipleship; he decided to be sure and follow up with anyone he led to Christ. "Don't bring spiritual babes to birth and leave them to die for lack of nourishment," he warned his fellow workers. He also had a growing conviction that he could minister more effectively by pouring into one life than by haphazardly trying to reach large groups without any consistency.

Soon, Dawson moved to San Diego to lead a ministry for Christian sailors in the Navy. He already had a heart for servicemen (his dad had worked in a shipyard when Dawson was growing up), and he often traveled to San Diego to lead a Bible study for them. Now he got closely connected with a serviceman named Les Spencer, who worked on the U.S.S. West Virginia. He began teaching Les to study the Bible, often inviting him over and spending lots of time with him.

Les grew excited about what he was learning from Dawson, and he wanted one of his shipmates to learn, too. But when he asked Dawson if he could bring the man over, Dawson's response was surprising: "You teach him," he said. When Les protested that he hadn't had any training, Dawson responded, "Doesn't matter. If you can't teach him what I've taught you, I've failed."

As Les grew in his faith, it spread to those around him. Soon, the first Service Men's Bible Club was born. Dawson began meeting with four sailors—Les, his friend Gurney Harris, and two others who were converted as a result of the meetings.

Before long, those original four servicemen were bringing their shipmates to Christ and discipling them, and those men were sharing their faith with new men. By 1934, the growing group was named "The Navigators: A Bible Club for Service Men" because of the parallels to navigation at sea. The West Virginia eventually had Bible classes nearly every night; it was even nicknamed "The Floating Seminary"! And when the United States joined World War II in 1941, men who had been trained through Dawson's work with the Navigators were sent out around the world.

Dawson continued to meet with the servicemen and minister to them, but when a serviceman won someone to Christ and asked Dawson to help him out, his response was, "What are you planning to do for him?" He challenged the one who had brought the person to Christ to help that new believer grow.

Dawson finally realized that he had been missing one key piece to the idea of follow-up: producing reproducers. Though servicemen were holding lots of Bible classes on their ships, they weren't doing enough man-to-man ministry. In order for all the men to be reached, Christians must start discipling men in order for them to be able to disciple others. "The one big challenge before The Navigators is to produce reproducers," Dawson said. "Who, because of you, is carrying on the Gospel of Christ?"

The value of one-on-one ministry was simple: teaching new Christians to "do as I do" gave the teacher credibility and gave the learner hope. The new Christian was simply imitating the faith of his friend, who was just a regular man practicing the things he was teaching. Dawson saw that this method was slow and challenging, but that ultimately, it was more beneficial than trying to reach large numbers of people all at once. Spiritual multiplication, he said, is "reaching the greatest number of people in the most effective way in the shortest possible time." He believed that if only Christians could be mobilized to make disciples, the world could be reached and the Great Commission fulfilled in one generation.

The Navigators' ministry didn't end with servicemen. The group began sending men overseas to teach evangelism, follow-up and Scripture memorization in other countries. "The entire world was populated as a result of God's command to Adam and Eve to be fruitful and multiply," Dawson said. "It makes sense that if Christians would be fruitful and multiply, the entire world could be evangelized."

Dawson Trotman died at age fifty in a drowning accident, as he held a girl up to save her life and lost his own in the process. But his ministry continues through The Navigators, a worldwide ministry organization that still uses one-on-one relationships and small group discipleship to fulfill Dawson's life motto: "To know Christ and make Him known."

> *"OH LORD, HELP ME BUILD MEN, STRONG, HOLY, PREPARED MEN TO GO TO THE FOUR CORNERS OF THE WORLD WHO WILL DO THE SAME."*

SIGNIFICANT CONTRIBUTION

Dawson Trotman reintroduced the church to the lost priority of disciple-making and spiritual reproduction. Today, the ministry he started is active around the world on college campuses, military bases, inner cities, prisons, and youth camps. The Navigators are continuing Dawson's legacy by teaching people "to follow Christ passionately by applying the Bible to their daily lives, passing on what they learn to others, and training these new believers to reach others."

FOCUS SCRIPTURE

"And the things you have heard me say in the presence of many witnesses entrust to reliable men who will also be qualified to teach others."(2 Timothy 2:2)

THINK ABOUT IT...

1. Read 2 Timothy 2:2. Paul instructed Timothy to pass on his teachings to "reliable men who will also be qualified to teach others." What makes a person reliable? What makes him or her qualified to teach others?

2. The concept of spiritual multiplication is based on the idea that deep relationships with fewer people can have a more powerful and lasting impact than one-time encounters with mass groups of people. Why do you think this is true?

3. Does the church in America value the hard work of one-one-one discipling and mentoring in the same way that Jesus did? Why or why not?

APPLY IT...

4. Dawson Trotman once said, "Remember, making a decision is 5 percent; 95 percent is following through. God is not glorified by a raised hand unless the decision is confirmed by a Christian life that follows it." What fruit can you identify in your own life to confirm that your faith is not just a one-time decision, but an ongoing walk with Christ?

5. Dawson heavily emphasized Scripture memory because of the positive impact it had on his own life and faith. What are some specific benefits to memorizing Scripture? Why does Scripture memorization seem to be a dying art in the church today? Set some realistic but challenging goals for memorizing Scripture and hiding God's Word in your heart.

6. The process of spiritual multiplication is not complete until the laborers you reproduce are also reproducing more laborers. If you are currently discipling someone, what steps can you take to encourage him or her to disciple others? If you are currently being discipled by someone, what do you need to do to be able to disciple others?

TAKE ACTION!

If you are not being discipled by anyone, start praying now and ask God to help you find a mentor. If you are already being discipled, ask God to lead you to someone who needs a mentor. (You could also ask your pastor or a friend for guidance in helping you find someone.) Tell someone who can pray along with you and hold you accountable to finding a mentoring relationship to help you grow.

THE LABORER'S DECLARATION

LIKE A RUNNER in the relay race of human history, I accept the baton of responsibility to reach my generation for Christ. I cannot live for today, thinking only of myself. I cannot pretend that the unreached are not lost, that hell is not real, or that I am not accountable for the needs around me.

Laborers from other generations have gone before me. They have taken their turn at using their gifts to build God's Kingdom. Today, I commit myself to join their ranks as a laborer in my generation, seeking to cultivate the Christlike characteristics and actions they displayed. It's my turn.

LOVE

1. I affirm that loving God is the foundation for all service to Him. It's my turn to love God intimately and deeply.

2. I affirm that the character of God is expressed to the world through unconditional love and sacrifice. It's my turn to sacrifice myself for God and others.

3. I affirm that loving others requires a servant's heart. It's my turn to serve others with humility.

4. I affirm that being a laborer will require a complete surrender to the Lordship of Christ. It's my turn to obey God with reckless abandon.

5. I affirm that we gain our lives only when we give them away. It's my turn to die to self.

6. I affirm the priority of prayer as the driving force behind all Kingdom advancement. It's my turn to intercede for the lost.

LIFE

7. I affirm that God has designed a lifestyle for me that demands supernatural power. It's my turn to live by faith.

8. I affirm that because the Word of God is my final authority, I must be different when the values of my culture contradict the values of the Kingdom. It's my turn to stand for truth.

9. I affirm that being a living sacrifice may bring persecution from others. It's my turn to share in Christ's suffering.

THE LABORER'S DECLARATION

10. I affirm that a life lived with Christ requires endurance to finish strong. It's my turn to run the race of faith with perseverance.

11. I affirm that God builds His Kingdom through ordinary people, not just a select few who have certain kinds of gifts and callings. It's my turn to advance the Kingdom by playing the role uniquely designed for me by God.

12. I affirm that I am accountable for everything God has given me. It's my turn to use my God-given gifts for His glory.

LEGACY

13. I affirm that only through Jesus can we have relationship with God and hope for eternity. It's my turn to share the Gospel with others in verbal and relational ways.

14. I affirm God's purpose to establish His church from all the peoples of the earth. It's my turn to bless the nations.

15. I affirm that the strategy of Jesus for world conquest is spiritual multiplication. It's my turn to reproduce other laborers through life-on-life mentoring.

Signature _____

Date _____

CONCLUSION

A FINAL WORD OF CAUTION

IT IS OUR PRAYER that you have progressed through the stories in this book and have wholeheartedly embraced "The Laborer's Declaration." But living out the "It's my turn" affirmation statements in that declaration won't always be easy. Every commitment must be followed by a process of growth if a believer is to bear fruit over the long haul. As Dawson Trotman said, "Remember, making a decision is 5 percent; 95 percent is following through. God is not glorified…unless the decision is confirmed by a Christian life that follows it."

We would like to leave you with a few practical suggestions to encourage you as you follow through on your commitment and take your place in the relay race of human history.

1. EXPECT OPPOSITION FROM THE ENEMY.

Your decision to be a committed laborer for God has not gone unnoticed by Satan. And when soldiers get closer to the front lines of battle, the fighting gets more intense. It's no different for the spiritual battle we're in—1 Peter 5:8 says, "Your enemy the devil prowls around like a roaring lion looking for someone to devour."

You have nothing to fear, because "the One who is in you is greater than the one who is in the world" (1 John 4:4). At the same time, it would be naive and foolish to ignore the reality of spiritual warfare. Satan would love to render you ineffective in the battle for human souls. Remember to put on the full armor of God each day (Ephesians 6:10-18). Trust in the love and grace of God and His Spirit at work within you. And know that He who has begun a good work in you will be faithful to complete it (Philippians 1:6)!

2. BEWARE OF THE "ELIJAH SYNDROME."

After the great victory on Mount Carmel over the prophets of Baal in 1 Kings 18, Elijah hit bottom. Jezebel threatened him, and he panicked, running for his life. All alone at Mount Horeb, Elijah poured out his soul before God. "I have been very zealous for the LORD God Almighty," he said. "The Israelites have rejected your covenant, broken down your altars, and put our prophets to death with the sword. I am the only one left, and now they are trying to kill me, too" (1 Kings 19:10).

Elijah was convinced that he was the only one who was faithful to God. Upon facing opposition, he bought into a lie that Satan has successfully used over and over again. You, too, may be tempted to look around you and believe that you are the only remaining faithful believer. But listen to God's perspective on Elijah's situation: "I reserve seven thousand in Israel—whose knees have not bowed down to Baal and whose mouths have not kissed him" (1 Kings 19:18).

In spite of how it may appear, you are not alone. Not only has God has placed His Holy Spirit within you, but He is also raising up laborers in every part of the world! Ask God to guide you to the like-minded laborers in your area. Encourage one another as you work together to build God's Kingdom.

3. DEAL WITH REJECTION GRACIOUSLY.

Some people will not understand the commitments you have made in "The Laborer's Declaration." Laborers from every generation have been branded as radicals and fanatics. Even members of your family, church, or campus group may find it difficult to accept your newfound zeal in pursuing God's purpose for your life.

The apostle Paul gives laborers of every generation some important words of instruction on this subject. In his second letter to the Corinthians, Paul listed many of the hardships he faced in the process of obedience. These included dishonor, bad reports, and being regarded as an impostor—all of this on top of imprisonment, beatings, and sleepless nights! But in this same passage, Paul emphasized the importance of "purity, understanding, patience...kindness and sincere love" (2 Corinthians 6:6). As you face rejection and misunderstanding, ask God to empower you with the fruit of the Holy Spirit. Eventually, those skeptics and critics may be won over by the grace and love they see portrayed in your life.

4. BALANCE YOUR ZEAL WITH WISDOM.

Clearly, passion is necessary in carrying out your commitment to be a laborer. Paul urged the church in Rome to be passionate, saying, "Never be lacking in zeal, but keep your spiritual fervor, serving the Lord" (Romans 12:11). The church today is in desperate need of zealous laborers—but at the other extreme, "it is not good to have zeal without knowledge, nor to be hasty and miss the way" (Proverbs 19:2).

Seek out godly counsel and other mature believers. Strive to grow and develop your ministry skills. Cooperate with existing ministry structures whenever possible. Season your words with love. And beware of alienating those around you by plowing ahead without first gaining wisdom.

5. GUARD YOUR HEART AGAINST PRIDE.

Making a sincere commitment to be a laborer will open the door of blessing on your life. Expect God to use you to advance His Kingdom! But as you begin to experience results, you may be tempted to take the credit or seek recognition for what you have accomplished. Beware—God will not share His glory with anyone. One of the most common stumbling blocks to fruitful Kingdom service is pride. Remember the words of Peter, who said, "God opposes the proud but gives grace to the humble. Humble yourselves, therefore, under God's mighty hand, that He may lift you up in due time" (1 Peter 5:5-6).

6. PERSEVERE EVEN WHEN YOUR EMOTIONS AREN'T HIGH.

One of the most common statements your skeptics will make is that your newfound vision and passion will never last. "It's just a fad," they might say. "Youthful zeal— wait and see." While it's true that your feelings will come and go, being a laborer is not about riding an emotional wave into heaven. Reality checks will come all too often—and sometimes, God has the most to teach us in the valleys of life, after we come down from those mountaintop experiences. When you don't feel those emotions in your relationship with God, it's a time for your faith to be refined as you persevere. Don't give up! Love and faith are more than just feelings.

Like thousands of others who have gone before you, you can persevere in your commitment to live a life of total surrender to the cause of Christ. By God's grace, you can stand against the force of a hostile culture that seeks to water down your vision.

7. DON'T LET FAILURE DISCOURAGE YOU FROM RUNNING THE RACE.

At one time or another, you will ask yourself, "What's the use?" And at some point, a moment of weakness may overtake you, and you will fail—perhaps miserably. But don't give up! Accept God's forgiveness and get back into the battle. Remember that when you are weak, His strength is made perfect (2 Corinthians 12:9). Draw upon the power of accountability relationships, considering how you can "spur one another on toward love and good deeds... all the more as you see the Day approaching" (Hebrews 10:24-25).

The road of Kingdom laborership may be tough, but if you keep your eyes fixed on Jesus and run the race with perseverance, you can one day take your place among the faithful "cloud of witnesses"—the laborers in this book and millions of others like them who have devoted their lives to the cause of Christ. You've remembered these leaders...you've considered the outcome of their way of life... now imitate their faith.

IT'S YOUR TURN!

APPENDIX A

WHAT IS A LABORER?

(adapted from "The World's Greatest Need" by Dwight Robertson)

AS JESUS TRAVELED from place to place, He was keenly aware of the profound needs of people all around Him. He was moved with compassion. At one point, He turned to His disciples and shared in one word what a world of hurting people needs most. This word represents His plan for meeting the greatest human needs.

"And Jesus went about all the cities and villages, teaching in their synagogues and preaching the gospel of the kingdom, and healing every disease and every infirmity. When he saw the crowds, he had compassion for them, because they were harassed and helpless, like sheep without a shepherd. Then he said to his disciples, 'The harvest is plentiful, but the laborers are few; pray therefore the Lord of the harvest to send out laborers into his harvest'" (Matthew 9:35-38 RSV, emphasis mine).

It's not a very glamorous word. It may not grab your attention, and it's certainly not a word you would see in a Madison Avenue advertising campaign. Still, it's the word Jesus chose.

What the world needs, Jesus said, is laborers. Common laborers. Jesus said the harvest is plentiful, but the laborers are few. He told us to pray that God would send laborers wherever there's human need.

In short, laborers aren't just critical to God's plan for the world. They are God's plan. And there's no Plan B.

HALLMARKS OF MINISTRY IN THE 20TH CENTURY

In recent years, we've been enamored with ministry activities that are in the spotlight and on the platform. The ministry heroes of the past few decades have been "Christian celebrities"—talented musicians, dynamic speakers, best-selling authors, powerful Christian leaders and well-known pastors. There has been no shortage of these kinds of heroes.

But "Christian celebrities" aren't the answer to the great harvest need. When the work is done, it will have been accomplished by nameless, faceless people who did what they could, where they were, with God adding the increase to their labor. God's work through ordinary laborers is what the world needs most. He's not calling just a few select people to make the difference. Instead, His plan is to mobilize an army of laborers who go into every place of human need.

Every one of us is called to be a laborer in this army. Every Christian has a significant role to play. From those who serve on the platform to those who serve in the hidden places. From those who serve with their mouths and minds, to those who serve with their hands and feet.

The Scripture is full of examples of ordinary laborers who had an extraordinary influence on those around them. Look at the 12 ordinary men Jesus chose to be His disciples. They weren't rabbis. They weren't the most brilliant scholars or the most charismatic speakers. They were a cross-section of ordinary people— fishermen, a tax collector, some businessmen. They're the kind of ordinary people Jesus still uses.

HALLMARKS OF A LABORER

Because the word laborer is not an everyday, household word, you might be wondering what exactly it means. As we've examined the whole of Scripture, we think a clear and simple definition emerges. A laborer is a disciple in action. Whereas the word disciple implies one who accepts a teaching and learns from a master, the word laborer takes it one step further, implying that this teaching is put into action.

But being a laborer isn't just about action. It's also about being—that is, being in a love relationship with Christ. In fact, the Bible seems to identify at least three characteristics that are hallmarks of a laborer.

LOVE

Laborers have an intimate love relationship with Jesus and a passion for bringing Him glory. They realize their intimacy with Jesus is the greatest thing they have to give to the world.

LIFE

Their deep relationship with Christ overflows in a life of distinct, personal ministry. This ministry is as unique as each laborer is. It may be ordinary and everyday stuff, but in the hands of God, its results can be truly extraordinary. Regardless of what the distinct ministry is, every true laborer is willing to roll up his or her sleeves and pant-legs and wade into the mud puddles of human need.

LEGACY

Laborers leave a lasting spiritual legacy by reproducing other Kingdom laborers like themselves. They make an impact on people's lives one life at a time. They take the Kingdom of God into places that it might, otherwise, not go. The results are eternal.

A laborer's life is like a drop of water in a lake. One drop causes a ripple effect that spreads out in every direction. Likewise, the circle of influence of one common laborer can be profound. And the circle of influence of an army of laborers can be world-changing.

None of these characteristics of a laborer require that you be in full-time, vocational ministry. Of course, some laborers will be—but it is crucial for most to stay in the marketplace at their jobs, functioning as fully devoted laborers for Christ. If we all would commit to becoming laborers where we live and to obeying His personal instruction to us, the task of the Great Commission could be fulfilled. Remember, this was Jesus' solution to the state of the world: Laborers.

The chapters in this book use examples from the lives of fifteen men and women who have gone before us in order to illustrate the characteristics of a laborer. We hope that the stories of their lives will help you to evaluate your own life as a laborer. Are you using your gifts in a strategic way? Can you point to how God's Kingdom is advancing because of your labor? Are you reproducing spiritually?

No matter where you are in your spiritual journey, you can become an active Kingdom laborer. You can move beyond sitting in the pew to and start serving in the harvest fields. As you read these biographies and learn about the characteristics of a laborer, we hope that you will be inspired to become a laborer and share in God's harvest.

Andrews, Mary Raymond Shipman. A Lost Commander: Florence Nightingale. New York: Doubleday, 1929.

Bainton, Roland. Here I Stand: A Life of Martin Luther. Nashville: Abingdon, 1978.

Belmonte, Kevin. William Wilberforce. Colorado Springs: NavPress, 2002.

Benge, Janet & Geoff. George Müller: The Guardian of Bristol's Orphans. Seattle: YWAM, 1999.

Day of Discovery: The Biography of Josiah Henson. Dir. Don Boyer. 60 min. RBC Ministries, 2005. Videocassette.

Brown, Pam. Florence Nightingale. Milwaukee: Gareth Stevens, 1989.

Elliot, Elisabeth. A Chance to Die: The Life and Legacy of Amy Carmichael. Grand Rapids: Baker, 1987.

Furneaux, Robin. William Wilberforce. London: Hamish Hamilton, 1974.

Galli, Mark, and Ted Olsen. 131 Christians Everyone Should Know. Nashville: Broadman & Holman, 2000.

George, Timothy. Faithful Witness: The Life and Mission of William Carey. Birmingham, Alabama: New Hope, 1991.

Green, Melody, and David Hazard. No Compromise: The Life Story of Keith Green. Chatsworth, California: Sparrow, 1989.

Grubb, Norman. C.T. Studd: Cricketer and Pioneer. Fort Washington, Pennsylvania: Christian Literature Crusade, 1994.

Harmon, Rebecca Lamar. Susanna, Mother of the Wesleys. Nashville: Abingdon, 1968.

Henson, Josiah. Father Henson's Story of His Own Life. Boston: Jewett, 1858.

Laurent, Bob. Watchman Nee: Man of Suffering. Ulrichsville, Ohio: Barbour, 1998.

McGaw, Francis. John Hyde: The Apostle of Prayer. Minneapolis: Bethany House, 1970.

McReynolds, Kathy. Susanna Wesley. Minneapolis: Bethany, 1998.

71545223R00053

Made in the USA
Middletown, DE
25 April 2018